The Poetry o

General

C. A. PATRIDES

Reader in English, University of York

John Milton

The Minor Poems in English

Introduction by

A. D. Nuttall

Reader in English, University of Sussex

Notes on the Text by

Douglas Bush

Professor of English, Harvard University

MACMILLAN

Published by
MACMILLAN EDUCATION LTD
Basingstoke and London

The Macmillan Company of Australia Pty Ltd Melbourne
The Macmillan Company of Canada Ltd Toronto
St Martin's Press Inc New York

Companies and representatives throughout the world

Printed in Great Britain by A. Wheaton & Co Exeter

Contents

Acknowledgements

An edition of Milton's poetry in several volumes necessarily draws on the talents of many critics and scholars. Our primary obligation in this volume is to Professor Douglas Bush, Houghton Mifflin Company, and Oxford University Press, for permission to use his annotation from *The Complete Poetical Works of John Milton* (Boston, 1965, and London, 1966); and to Professor John T. Shawcross and Doubleday and Co. Inc., for permission to reprint his text from *The Complete English Poetry of John Milton* (New York, 1963). Additionally the University of Texas Press has allowed me to quote from Harry J. Leon's translations in *The Pastoral Elegy: An Anthology*, ed. T. P. Harrison (Austin, 1939).

The principal contributors to the several volumes were not required to conform to any restrictive guidelines: the introductions were left entirely to their discretion. The notes and appendices, however, were submitted for their approval.

The original spelling used in Professor Shawcross's edition is here modernised with due regard paid to scansion, unnecessary initial capital letters are reduced and unnecessary italics are eliminated.

For general advice I am grateful to J. B. Bamborough, Provost of Linacre College, Oxford; Professor David Daiches of the University of Sussex; and Dame Helen Gardner, Merton Professor of English Literature at Oxford.

My final debt of gratitude is to Mr A. D. Nuttall who provides the introduction to the present volume. At his request, the text of the 'Minor Poems' has been augmented by the addition of Milton's translation of the Fifth Ode of Horace. The dates given in each instance adhere to the chronology provided by Professor Bush.

C.A.P.

An Outline
of Milton's Life

within the context of contemporary events

☙☙☙☙☙☙☙☙☙☙☙☙☙☙☙☙☙☙☙☙☙☙☙☙☙☙☙☙☙☙☙☙☙☙☙☙

The Reign of James I

1603 24 Mar: death of Elizabeth I; accession of James I
1608 9 Dec: John Milton born in Bread Street, Cheapside, London
1612 Death of Henry, Prince of Wales
1616 Death of Shakespeare
1618 Execution of Sir Walter Ralegh
1620 Settlement of first New England colony by the Pilgrim Fathers
1620? Milton attends St. Paul's School (to 1624)
1621 Andrew Marvell born
1625 12 Feb: Milton admitted to Christ's College, Cambridge; matriculated on 9 April

   27 Mar: death of James I; accession of Charles I

The Reign of Charles I

1625 Outbreak of the plague
1626 Death of Sir Francis Bacon
1629 26 Mar: Milton admitted to the Degree of Bachelor of Arts
1630 Prince Charles (later Charles II) born
1631 Death of John Donne
1632 3 July: Milton admitted to the Degree of Master of Arts. His poem 'On Shakespeare' published in the Second Folio of Shakespeare's plays. Resides at Hammersmith with family (to 1635?)

1633 William Laud appointed Archbishop; demands conformity
        against mounting opposition
1634 29 Sept: *A Mask* [*Comus*] performed
1635? Milton resides at Horton, Buckinghamshire, with family
        (to 1638)
1637 *A Mask* [*Comus*] published
        3 April: death of Milton's mother
        Death of Ben Jonson
1638 *Lycidas* published in a memorial volume to Edward King;
        April (?): Milton embarks on a visit to France and Italy
1639 War with Scotland
        Milton returns to London in the late summer, tutors privately
            (to about 1647); resides first at St Bride's Churchyard, then
            at Aldersgate Street (to 1645)
1641 The Long Parliament convenes
        Laud is impeached and imprisoned
        Milton engaged in the war of the pamphlets concerning the
            episcopal form of ecclesiastical government; his five anti-
            prelatical tracts begin with *Of Reformation*, probably in May;
            Of Prelatical Episcopacy, in June or July; and *Animadversions*,
            in July
        Execution of Strafford
        Irish Rebellion
        The 'Grand Remonstrance' issued
1642 Milton publishes two more anti-prelatical tracts, *The Reason
            of Church Government*, in January or February, and *An
            Apology*, in April
        Parliamentary strength increases; Charles I removes to Oxford.
        June (?): Milton marries Mary Powell; she returns to her
            father's home, probably in August
        22 Aug: Charles I raises his standard at Nottingham; the
            Civil War begins
1643 'Solemn League and Covenant': Parliament undertakes to
        reform the church

1 Aug: Milton publishes the first of four divorce tracts, *The Doctrine and Discipline of Divorce*

1644   Parliamentary victory at Marston Moor

Milton publishes *Of Education* in June, and *Areopagitica* in November; the second divorce tract, *The Judgement of Martin Bucer*, published in August

1645   Execution of Laud

Rise of the New Model Army; Parliamentary victories at Naseby and elsewhere

March: Milton publishes the last two divorce tracts, *Tetrachordon* and *Colasterion*

Summer (?): Mary Powell returns to Milton; they reside at Barbican (to 1647)

Autumn (?): 1st edition of *The Poems of Mr John Milton* ('The Minor Poems')

1646   29 July: birth of Milton's first daughter Anne

1647   13 Mar (?): death of Milton's father

Aug: Parliamentary army occupies London

Milton resides at High Holborn (to 1649)

Charles I is arrested; escapes

1648   Second Civil War; Charles I is seized

25 Aug: birth of Milton's second daughter Mary

1649   30 Jan: execution of Charles I

Charles II, proclaimed in Scotland, escapes to France in 1651

The Interregnum

1649   Feb: Milton endorses regicide in *The Tenure of Kings and Magistrates*

15 Mar: Milton appointed Secretary of Foreign Tongues to the Council of State (to 1659?); resides first at Charing Cross, then at Scotland Yard, Westminster (to 1651)

Cromwell in Ireland

Oct: Milton at the order of the Council of State writes and

publishes *Eikonoklastes* ('The Image Breaker') in reply to *Eikon Basilike* ('The Royal Image'), attributed to Charles I

1650   Milton issues enlarged editions of *The Tenure of Kings and Magistrates* and *Eikonoklastes*

His blindness progresses rapidly

1651   Feb: Milton at the order of the Council of State writes and publishes *Pro populo anglicano defensio* (the so-called 'First Defence of the English People') in reply to Salmasius's defence of Charles I (1649)

16 Mar: birth of Milton's first son John; the family move to Petty France, Westminster (to 1660)

Hobbes's *Leviathan* published

1652   End of war in Ireland

Milton's blindness becomes total

2 May: birth of Milton's third daughter Deborah

5 May (?): death of his wife Mary

15 June (?): death of his son John

1653   The Protectorate established under Cromwell

1654   May: Milton at the order of the Council of State writes and publishes *Defensio secunda pro populo anglicano* ('The Second Defence of the English People') in reply to Pierre du Moulin's attack on the Commonwealth (1652)

1655   Aug: Milton publishes *Pro se defensio* ('Defence of Himself') in reply to a personal attack by Alexander More (1654)

1656   12 Nov: Milton marries Katherine Woodcock

1657   Sept (?): Andrew Marvell appointed Milton's assistant in the Secretaryship

19 Oct: birth of Milton's fourth daughter Katherine

1658   3 Feb: death of Milton's second wife Katherine

17 Mar: death of his daughter Katherine

3 Sept: death of Cromwell; the Protectorate passes to his son Richard

1659   Milton publishes *A Treatise of Civil Power* in February, and

Considerations touching the likeliest means to remove Hirelings out of the Church in August

25 May: Richard Cromwell obliged to abdicate; the Protectorate ends

1660 Feb: Milton publishes *The Ready and Easy Way to Establish a Free Commonwealth*

29 May: Charles II, recalled by Parliament, enters London

The Restoration

1660 Milton imprisoned for a time; copies of his books burned by order of Parliament

The theatres, closed since 1642, re-opened

The Royal Society founded

1661 Milton after a brief stay at Holborn, resides at Jewin Street (to 1663)

1662 'Act of Uniformity'

1663 24 Feb: Milton marries Elizabeth Minshull; they reside at Artillery Walk, Bunhill Fields (to 1674)

1664 Autumn: outbreak of the Great Plague (to early 1666); Milton moves temporarily to Chalfont St Giles, Bucks.

1666 Sept: London devastated by fire

1667 Aug (?): *Paradise Lost* published

1669 June (?): Milton's *Accidence Commenc't Grammar* published

1670 Nov (?): Milton's *History of Britain* published

1671 Feb (?): *Paradise Regained* and *Samson Agonistes* published jointly (2nd edition, posthumously in 1680)

1672 May (?): Milton's *Artis Logicae Plenior Institutio* ('A Fuller Institution of the Art of Logic') published

1673 May (?): Milton's *Of True Religion, Heresy, Schism and Toleration* published

Nov (?): 2nd enlarged edition of the 'Minor Poems' (1645)

1674 May: Milton's *Epistolae Familiares et Prolusiones* ('Letters and Prolusions') published

July: 2nd revised edition of *Paradise Lost*

Death of Milton about 8 November; buried in St Giles,
Cripplegate, on 12 November

Milton's posthumously published works include in particular his Latin
treatise on Christian doctrine, *De Doctrina Christiana* (discovered
in 1823, first published in 1825)

Introduction

𝔊𝔊𝔊𝔊𝔊𝔊𝔊𝔊𝔊𝔊𝔊𝔊𝔊𝔊𝔊𝔊𝔊𝔊𝔊𝔊𝔊𝔊𝔊𝔊𝔊𝔊𝔊𝔊𝔊𝔊𝔊𝔊𝔊𝔊𝔊𝔊𝔊𝔊

I

Most literary revolutions can be described as a return to nature. The very different ways in which Donne and Wordsworth transformed poetry can both be called reaction against artifice. But Milton, unquestionably one of the greatest revolutionaries in the history of literature, had a different idea. His cry, instead of being 'Back to nature!' was 'Back to books!' He revolted against the practice of his own day in order to find a harsher discipline than his own times could offer. His objection to his literary environment was not that it was restricting, but that it was too lax. Like Shakespeare's Isabella in *Measure for Measure*, he spoke

> not as desiring more
> But rather wishing a more strict restraint.
> (I.iv.3–4)

He therefore trained himself, with all the rigour of a modern athlete, on Greek, Latin, Hebrew and Italian literature, and rapidly passed from imitation to emulation. No literature was too difficult for Milton, though several were rejected as too easy. Milton was thus a deeply traditional rebel.

But the second thing we learn about Milton is that he had no followers. It is true that imitation of Milton was fashionable in the eighteenth century, but Addison, who published in 1704 a translation from Virgil entitled *Milton's style imitated*, is not really evidence of a Miltonic tradition in the way that Marvell is of Donne's. Odd tricks of Miltonic phrasing recur in poets as different as Collins and Keats, but, when successful, what they evoke is not the mature but the early Milton (most of all *Comus*) and in the early Milton the features on which they fasten are seldom the most distinctively Miltonic. The efforts of those who chose to imitate *Paradise Lost* were not happy. The truth is that Milton was too learned. A new sort of directness, of truth to evident facts, can be picked up by a clever man in a matter of hours. The power of organising three ancient literatures and two modern into a powerful and coherent body of poetry is less easily communicated.

Milton emerges from all this as a sort of literary freak. Instead of destroying the old in order to construct the new, he carefully dried up the sources of innovation in order to revive what was ancient and authoritative. He strangely reverses Freud's picture of primitive human nature. Milton does not begin his period of power by killing his father; instead, he strenuously killed off, one by one, all his unborn children.

His art was harshly retrospective. The vivid, the brilliant, the sensuous, the immediate, the specific were gradually extirpated from his verse. Lines which might have begotten scores of imitations, such as:

> Walks in black vapours, though the noontide brand
> Blaze in the summer solstice

were scratched out in manuscript and remoter, drabber lines substituted—in this case:

> Benighted walks under the midday sun;
> Himself is his own dungeon.

It is arguable that in the end Milton carried his surgery too far and sacrificed his patient's life. Certainly most readers prefer the imperfectly repressed splendours of *Comus* to the too-perfect austerity of *Paradise Regained*. *Paradise Lost*, which was written between *Comus* and *Paradise Regained*, owes much of its power to a recalcitrant sensuousness. Milton's classical asceticism is heroic in its effect, but only as long as its mastery is incomplete.

All this involves, as I have implied, a certain harsh negativity. Milton's stylistic development can certainly be seen as a series of abstentions. The notion of poetic austerity has, perhaps, unpleasant associations for the twentieth century, which likes to think of itself as life-affirming, yet I suspect that in this respect Milton anticipates the modern age. Anyone who has tried to write poetry in our own time knows how the process of composition is largely taken up with rejection of lines that will not do: 'No—that's not it—cross it out, and try again.' Even where an author is fluent enough to avoid many re-writings, we feel that a large element of his success consists in knowing what *not* to include. One has no such sense in contemplating the work of Brueghel, or Shakespeare, or Chaucer. For them, one feels, art consisted in *making*, in adding, filling out, completing. This is not to say that the work of older artists has no standards of relevance. Chaucer knows very well when ribaldry is inadmissible. But one feels that the irrelevant presented him with few problems. It did not clamour for inclusion. He did not need, as the modern needs, an unremitting vigilance against the intrusion of the commonplace, the cliché, the off-key. E. H. Gombrich has contrasted[1] the fluent sketches of a mediaeval artist such as Villard d'Honnecourt with the multitudinous re-workings and rejected forms of Leonardo's Renaissance notebooks. In applying this to Milton we are not merely guessing at mental processes which can never be checked. His austerity of diction is clear enough. Anyone who reads the *Amoretti* of Spenser, or the more varied sonnets of Drayton, and then turns to Milton's sonnets will see that much is admitted by the early poets which is excluded by Milton.

But the very appositeness of Gombrich's comparison of d'Honnecourt with Leonardo da Vinci does perhaps cast doubt on the uniqueness of Milton's learned and self-critical revolution. The difference between the two draughtsmen is a form of the difference between the

[1] 'Leonardo's method for Working out Compositions', in his *Norm and Form* London, 1966 pp. 58–63

Middle Ages and the Renaissance. And what was the Renaissance, if not a bookish revolution, a self-conscious yet defiant submission to the disciplines of antiquity?

The Renaissance, as everyone knows, differs from the Middle Ages in that it presided at its own christening. It was a self-announcing movement. Petrarch, Vespasiano, Boccaccio, Lorenzo Valla, Vasari, all drew on metaphors of rebirth and resurrection to describe the artistic development they witnessed. The aspect of the Renaissance which is most relevant to Milton is humanism. By the term 'human-ism' we must understand, not 'the mystical ideal of human nobility'[1] (though this can certainly be found in Renaissance authors) but its technical meaning, 'the study of the grammar, rhetoric, history, poetry and moral philosophy of the ancient Greeks and Romans'. Milton would appear to be a straightforward instance of all this.

II

There are however two objections to describing Milton as a Renais-sance humanist. The first is that Milton comes too late for the English Renaissance, of which the typical figures were Spenser and Shakespeare; the second is that he is even further removed from humanism which in English cultural history is separable from the main literary renaissance, and which in fact, in such figures as Erasmus, Sir Thomas More and Sir John Cheke (who introduced the Erasmian pronunciation of Greek into the University of Cambridge) preceded the golden age of Elizabethan verse.

As for the first objection, although it is too late to alter a well-established usage, I would dispute the propriety of describing Shake-speare and Spenser as Renaissance figures. The most useful meaning of

---

[1] See Augustin Renaudet *Humanisme et Renaissance, Travaux d'Humanisme et Renaissance*, XXX, Geneva, 1958 p. 35

'renaissance' is that suggested by its etymology: 'rebirth'. The word thus connotes a turning point; and more than this, the bringing back to life of something which has already lived once. What is revived in a new form is, of course, the ancient civilisation of Greece and Rome. Now it is an interesting fact that Englishmen find it easy to doubt the very existence of the Renaissance, to argue that nothing really important was created by the revivers, but that on the contrary they simply neglected and despised the genuinely valuable elements in their mediaeval heritage. As C. S. Lewis put it (speaking specifically of Renaissance humanism, but the remark is symptomatic of his attitude to the Renaissance as a whole), 'Before they ceased talking of a rebirth it became evident that they had really built a tomb.'[1] As long as one remains in England this view is credible. The transition from Gothic to classical forms in architecture is in England gradual and happily muddled. There is no great moment of powerful and lucid assertion. Although in literature there was without doubt a great flowering in the second half of the sixteenth century, the poetry of Shakespeare and Spenser resembles the architecture of the period in showing no great urge to sever relations with the past but rather a loving and intimate regard for it. Even Ben Jonson, who did have the conscious Renaissance desire to reform literature in accordance with ancient rules, produced dramas which are richly compounded of Latin and mediaeval elements, of the Roman comedy and the English morality. Hence, perhaps, the persuasiveness to English ears of Lewis's view.

But one has only to spend a day walking about the streets of Florence to have one's faith in the reality of the Renaissance renewed. Again and again, one turns a corner, or passes through a church door, to find one's eye challenged by the wonderful lucidity of an architecture which has been born again. The Renaissance is primarily an Italian phenomenon. To learn about its nature one must go to Italy,

[1] *English Literature in the Sixteenth Century, Excluding Drama* London, 1954 p. 21

and, in Italy, to Florence. Once in Florence, one begins to see what the primary characteristics of Renaissance art are. The first illusion to be dispelled is the notion that the sensuous glorification of the human body is the essence of Renaissance art. In comparison with the late mediaeval art which preceded it, Renaissance painting is austere and, in a way, deliberately conceptual, preoccupied more with the mathematical analysis of spatial relations than with savouring the sensuous particular, with the unalterable laws of geometry rather than with the fluctuations of light effects on human skin. In the history of Renaissance art line precedes colour, Florence precedes Venice.

Thus the modern tendency to see this movement in terms of a renewed delight in the senses contrasting with mediaeval asceticism in fact reverses the real ideals of the revolution. Boccaccio praised Giotto on the ground that he

> brought back to light that art that had been buried for centuries under the errors of those who painted rather to delight the eyes of the ignorant than to please the intellect of the wise.[1]

Michelangelo condemned the proliferation of sensuous detail in Flemish painting and insisted that pictures should consist as far as possible of idealised human figures disposed in an indeterminate environment.

The next thing we learn about the Renaissance does far less violence to our preconceptions. It is that the sense of the artist himself as an individual, an imperious and distinctive personality, becomes much stronger. The Middle Ages can perhaps rival the works of Cellini, Leonardo and Michelangelo, but can hardly rival their recorded eccentricities.

If then the three main characteristics of the Renaissance are (1) an ostentatiously revolutionary revival of ancient forms, (2) a deliberate

---

[1] Quoted in E. H. Gombrich *Meditations on a Hobby Horse* London, 1963 p. 17

austerity in submission to these forms, involving the renunciation at many points of pleasing sensuous detail, and (3) a sense of a violent and distinctive personality manifesting itself in art—it seems clear that Spenser and Shakespeare are not truly Renaissance figures at all. These features are present in Ben Jonson, and it follows that he is a Renaissance poet. But it is in Milton that they coexist with the greatest intensity. There is only one real analogy in English literature to the personal *terribilità* of Michelangelo.

The other objection to our setting up Milton as the prime example of Renaissance humanism was that the humanist movement had run its course some seventy years before. This is in its way perfectly fair. But More and Erasmus and their associates carried out only the first stage of their Renaissance. The great monuments of their era are More's *Utopia* and Erasmus's *In Praise of Folly*. Both, significantly, are in Latin. It is true that certain of the Tudor humanists were interested in the problem of what could be done in the vernacular, not least Sir John Cheke himself, but they did not succeed in integrating the revival of Classical learning with the main body of written English. Literature differed from architecture and painting in that it was faced by a language barrier. The literary Renaissance falls, therefore, into two stages: first, the revival of a real linguistic understanding of Greek and Latin literature; then the translation of that knowledge into the vernacular culture. We may thus divide the humanists into primary and secondary, according as they precede or follow the passing of the language barrier. Milton is our greatest secondary humanist, and, in a profound sense, the supreme translator, not just of particular poems, but of whole cultures. That he saw himself as working in the humanist tradition is strongly suggested by the close of his eleventh sonnet ('A book was writ of late call'd *Tetrachordon*'):

Thy age, like ours, O soul of Sir John Cheek,
  Hated not learning worse than toad or asp,
    When thou taught'st Cambridge, and King Edward Greek.

III

Nevertheless it must be conceded that Milton was born rather late for a Renaissance artist. This is a point of substance because Milton's late arrival did mean that, even if there had been no true Renaissance revolution in England, the environment against which he reacted was not like Brunelleschi's or Leonardo's. For them the issue seemed comparatively simple: reaction against the undisciplined picturesqueness of the Middle Ages, great men against little men. Milton's situation, on the contrary, could hardly have been more inauspicious. He was born into the generation following the greatest English poet, perhaps the greatest of all poets. It is not easy to transport oneself imaginatively into a past epoch, but I would guess that a young poet following Shakespeare might feel singularly desolate. What, after this, was there left to do?

Milton immersed himself in the centrifugal, generous plenitude of Shakespeare's genius. Then he read and re-read the ancient authors. Then he knew what he must do: renounce, concentrate, elevate. The first of these terms has already been, to some extent, discussed. The second is best understood from examples; read *Antony and Cleopatra* and then, without pausing, begin on *Samson Agonistes*. The third, perhaps, needs both explanation and defence. In the twentieth century, we tend to admire a given book or poem for one of two reasons; we praise either the rich immediacy of sensuous experience, or else the mystery, the enigmatic ambiguity of what we read. But the great contribution of the Renaissance to literature is neither of these things. All the words we have to describe it have fallen into disrepute: dignity, decorum, elevation, idealisation; so far so, that the merits of Raphael, for four hundred years acknowledged to be one of the two or three greatest painters, have become almost invisible to us. It is only after seeing a great many pictures that we begin to know how far the subsequent history of art has been parasitic on Raphael. Certain majestic dispositions of the human body recur in painters as various as Rubens, Manet, Van Gogh, Poussin and Ingres. Manet's *Déjeuner sur l'Herbe* is a good example, since in it we can isolate the element of dignified elevation we are seeking. The picture shows with great realism two fully clothed nineteenth-century gentlemen and one plump, naked, nineteenth-century lady, sitting on the ground having a picnic. The position of the figures is taken from an engraving by Marcantonio after a painting by Raphael. Manet's picture, in contrast with Raphael's, is ironic, experiential; it asks us to notice and comment on the difference between the clothed and the unclothed figures, even to wonder whether the lady will catch cold. Raphael's picture clearly bore no such intimate relation to ordinary experience. It demanded only that we defer to the authority of the pose, recognise that here are formal relationships, which unlike those in a painting by Brueghel could not have been otherwise than they are.

Thus one might say that Manet's picture is a satire on Raphael's; by translating academic frigidity into vivid realism he has exposed its inadequacy. But such an account is superficial. Raphael does not merely provide Manet with material for satire; he also provides him with a great, magisterial composition. At the deepest level Manet accepts the authority of his master. Thus no account in terms of experiential details will ever explain the classic status of the painting. It owes that status to the very decorum which it pretends to deride.[1]

It is quite clear that Milton from the start felt the need of the literary equivalent of such central classic norms of utterance. He tried at first to find them in his native tradition of English, and apparently brought to the study of Shakespeare, Spenser, Jonson, and Fletcher the sort of studious attention normally reserved for antiquity. He seems to have been the first poet to be clearly aware that he was part of 'Eng. Lit.'. There is something incongruous in the application of the

[1] Rembrandt, who began by deriding the great Renaissance masters, but ended by accepting their authoritative schemata, is an interesting parallel. See Sir Kenneth Clark's *Rembrandt and the Italian Renaissance* London, 1966.

humanist method to such material. Milton went to these poets, one guesses, hoping to have his youthful genius disciplined and directed, but was embarrassed by the very generosity of his chosen authorities. He is like some children (they cannot be numerous) who secretly wish their parents would occasionally say no to their requests. What he required was not the rules for *genre*, that is the rules for writing a masque or a tragedy, so much as patterns of poetic *diction* which would stamp a work with a suprapersonal authority. He soon realised that he must look elsewhere for such abstract standards and methods. The selection of poems in this volume covers roughly the period of Milton's stylistic preparation for his great epic. To describe these poems in chronological order is to describe Milton's quest for high decorum. The minor poems afford an astonishing view of his stylistic workshop, but also, in *Lycidas*, an example of the successful completion of the quest, of what it was all about. *Lycidas* first appears in a collection of poems in memory of one Edward King, published in 1638. It is interesting to compare the opening of Milton's contribution with those of King, Beaumont and Cleveland.[1] Henry King's poem begins as follows:

> No death! I'll not examine God's decree,
> Nor question providence, in chiding thee:
> Discreet religion binds us to admire
> The ways of providence, and not enquire.

Joseph Beaumont begins:

> When first this news, rough as the sea
> From whence it came, began to be
> Sigh'd out by fame, and general tears

---

[1] For a detailed discussion of this, see David Daiches *Milton*, London, 1957 pp. 73f; also available in *Lycidas: the Tradition and the Poem* ed. C. A. Patrides, New York, 1961 pp. 101f.

> Drown'd him again, my stupid fears
> Would not awake; ...

And Cleveland:

> I like not tears in tune; nor will I prize
> His artificial grief, that scans his eyes:
> Mine weep down pious beads: but why should I
> Confine them to the Muse's rosary?
> I am not poet here; my pen's the spout
> Where the rainwater of my eyes run out
> In pity of that name, whose fate we see
> Thus copied out in grief's hydrography.

King's second couplet, with its foretaste of the polite Christianity of the eighteenth century, is less good than his first. Beaumont's lines, stressing first the pathetic fallacy which unites the weather with the news, and then his own exclusion from this cosmic sympathy, are almost powerful. Cleveland shows himself a competent metaphysical poet. Indeed all three openings are quite obviously by men who know what they are doing. This is the decent ground-bass of seventeenth-century poetry—intelligent, flexible, linguistically sensitive. And then we read (it is the last poem in the collection):

> Yet once more, O ye laurels, and once more
> Ye myrtles brown, with ivy never sere,
> I come to pluck your berries harsh and crude,
> And with forc'd fingers rude
> Shatter your leaves before the mellowing year ...

and we seem to be breathing a different air. How, we feel, could they bind those poems in the same volume as this?

Yet in what does this immeasurable superiority consist? If one wished to disparage Cleveland's poem one might say that the conceit of the rosary is a little tired, that Donne would have concentrated more ideas into less space. But this does nothing to explain why Milton is better than Cleveland. There is *less* play of intelligence in Milton's opening than in Cleveland's. Milton has not beaten the metaphysical poet at his own game. Rather he has disdained to play the game at all. Similarly with Beaumont: Milton's opening does not really surpass Beaumont's either in sensuous vigour or in psychological depth. There is no easy answer. It is something to do with the measured diction, with the play of sense units against line lengths, with the intensely dramatic yet controlled delay set up by the suspended line:

> And with forc'd fingers rude . . .

Milton has achieved the heroic inevitability of classic verse. The nature of that inevitability still eludes definition. The same problem confronts the historian of Renaissance art. Raphael was not a better *technician* than Van Eyck.

However we may sneer at notions like 'elevation' it is clear that Milton's heightening of pastoral diction was a radical development. In ancient Sicily Theocritus had written, for sophisticated Alexandrian readers, poems of the shepherd's life, often softening the native crudity of his material in order to give an oblique survey of fashionable literary squabbles, but often, too, catching the real sun-scorched ethos of rural Sicily. From Theocritus pastoral poetry passed to Virgil who transformed it into a sort of dreamlike projection of subjective preoccupations, amatory, literary or even political. From Virgil the line runs through Petrarch and Boccaccio, through Sannazaro who wished to recapture the pre-Virgilian simplicity, through didactic Mantuan who wanted no such thing, to England and Edmund Spenser. Some readers believe that the true business of pastoral poetry is to convey the felt atmosphere of rural life. For them Virgil is, or ought to be, the villain of the tradition. They feel the genre is impoverished by too close an adherence to academic authority; how can the poet see the trees and the grass before his eyes if his head is full of

Corydon and Alexis? Their sympathies will be with Sannazaro and Johann Heinrich Voss who sought to go behind Virgil and write directly of places they knew, Naples and Germany. Such an approach, however, will always go against the grain of pastoral form, which has built into it from the beginning certain ironies, certain kinds of sophisticated double-think which are scarcely compatible with the simple celebration of nature. Even Theocritus, as I have said, while he wrote *about* shepherds, wrote *for* a very different sort of person, and the nature of his audience conditioned the nature of his work. Throughout pastoral, alongside the admiration for rural simplicity, runs an aristocratic contempt for boorishness. Egalitarian sentiments are indulged but the poetry is misunderstood as long as these are respected as serious assertions. Such sentiments are all part of an essentially transient game of 'Let's pretend'. In the pastoral part of Shakespeare's *The Winter's Tale*, Perdita says:

> The self-same sun that shines upon his court
> Hides not his visage from our cottage, but
> Looks on alike.
>
> (IV.iv.451–3)

The Jacobean audience knew better than to take such radicalism too seriously; it knew in its heart that Perdita was in fact (though she did not realise it) of noble birth and would marry a noble husband; the ending was to be a real happy ending with no levelling nonsense. Pastoral was always devious in its relation to reality. It is no accident that it is a form which Wordsworth could never use.

But there are two spheres of reality to be considered: first the objective reality of flocks, shepherds and out-door weather, second the subjective reality of the poet's mind. It seems that those poets who acknowledge the deviousness of pastoral form, who deliberately encrust their work with ancient verbal ceremony win from the subjective sphere at least as much as they lose from the objective. It may be that in Virgil and Milton the objective pastoral fades into allegory, but we should remember that the very word 'allegory' implies the rise of a new meaning beneath the surface.

Spenser, clearly, thought that pastoral was, before all else, poetry of the shepherd's life. Accordingly, he studied his models and decided that the truest imitation of antiquity consisted not in the borrowing of classical names but in the discovery of good, earthy English equivalents. And indeed his case is at first sight very persuasive. A name like Daphnis cannot have sounded 'classical' to Theocritus as 'Lycidas' sounded to Milton. But how did the Greek name 'Amaryllis' sound to Virgil, who spoke Latin? Already the Latin poet has chosen to preserve the remote, Greek name. But Spenser will have none of this. His names are mere English: Diggon Davie, Colin Clout, Cuddie,Willye, Hobbinoll.

Spenser has made his choice, and the result is an admirable example of language from which all elevation has been removed:

> *Hobbinoll*   Diggon Davie! I bidde her god day!
>   Or Diggon her is, or I missaye.
> *Diggon*   Her was her, while it was daye light,
>   But now her is a most wretched wight etc.

It is a curious fact that by the critical standards of Wordsworth's Preface to *Lyrical Ballads* this ought to be true poetry. It is certainly the voice of 'a man speaking to men', 'the real language' of 'low and rustic life'. Spenser has indeed followed the precepts of Wordsworth's Preface more closely than Wordsworth ever did. And this ramshackle diction is the result. Dr Johnson described these lines as 'studied barbarity'. The phrase is perhaps more exact than is generally recognised. Spenser, as his prefatory epistle to Harvey makes clear, has deliberately lowered his language, has studiously devised this uncouth garb. His success is only too complete. 'Barbarity' is today as unpopular a term as 'elevation', yet (glance again at the opening of *Lycidas*) barbarous it is. The aristocratic schizophrenia of pastoral has vanished. Milton, when he tried the experiment of working with a rugged native vocabulary, was able to communicate the proper sense of tension between rusticity and refinement. But Spenser's rusticity is merely rustic, and as such has little to do with true pastoral. Virgil perceived that the tension of pastoral could hardly be achieved without reference to the alien, the remote. He read in Polybius that the shepherds in Arcadia held singing competitions, and made Arcadia his spiritual landscape.[1] He knew very well that his *Georgics*, in which he celebrated the husbandry of Italy, were not pastoral, but that his *Eclogues* were. Similarly, for Milton, 'Edward King' is not pastoral, but 'Lycidas' is.

The development of pastoral is only an exceptionally rich instance of the whole development of elevated poetic diction. Poets, consciously or unconsciously, came to realise that the heroic pitch could scarcely be achieved without interbreeding of native and ancient strains. Even a romantic like Blake implicitly acknowledged this truth in his line:

> Could frame thy fearful symmetry

where the Saxon immediacy of 'fearful' breaks against the formal severity of the Classical word 'symmetry'.

The aim of this introduction has so far been to win, if possible, some sympathy for Milton's self-imposed task, the elevation of English poetic diction. We can now turn to the actual poems which Milton wrote before *Paradise Lost* and try to see how he went about his work, how he experimented, and with what success. Lack of space compels me to confine my critical account pretty closely to five cardinal poems, *On the Morning of Christ's Nativity*, *L'Allegro*, *Il Penseroso*, *Comus* and *Lycidas*.

[1] See Bruno Snell *The Discovery of the Mind* Harper Torchbooks, New York, 1960 pp. 281-309.

IV

On the Morning of Christ's Nativity is Milton's first important work.
It is not a good poem but only a good poet could have written it. A
clue to its general tone is given by the beginning of the third stanza
of the first part:

> Say heav'nly Muse, shall not thy sacred vein
> Afford a present to the infant God?

The phrase which really sticks in the throat is 'infant God'. The fact
that 'God' is printed with a capital G is not much help. It takes a
moment to realise that Milton means the Christ-child, baby Jesus.
It is clear that this poem is to be an exercise in humanism. I do not
know whether Milton deliberately chose for his experiment the most
unsuitable material he could find. Certainly this exhumed apparatus
of Muses, Pan and Cynthia is scarcely applicable to such a subject
as the first Christmas. So many things which one would expect to
find in such a poem—a sense of the saving paradox of incarnation, of
the purging love of God come down into a wintry world in the body
of a helpless baby, of that pathos and majesty which together mark the
figure of Christ both at his nativity and at his crucifixion—simply are
not there. In his poem *On Shakespeare* Milton strangely transformed
the life-giving energy of Shakespeare into a Gorgon power of turning
men to monumental stone. One can come away from the Nativity
Ode feeling that he has done something very similar to Christ's
life-giving incarnation. The poem throws a strange light without
warmth. Milton's Christ is still-born.

Whenever the force of the traditional material seems likely to
burst through, Milton is swift to repress it. A critical description of
the poem in terms of these great inherited images can make it sound
very powerful. But criticism is not doing its job if it fails to point out

how Milton again and again petrifies his material. Milton read in the
Bible that when after the Great Flood a dove brought a spray of olive
to the Ark the waters ebbed and peace was restored. He also read in
his New Testament how the Spirit descended in the form of a dove
onto the head of Christ at his baptism. This pair of images obviously
possesses great potential power. In the Nativity Ode they appear as:

> But he her fears to cease,
> Sent down the meek-ey'd Peace;
>   She crown'd with olive green, came softly sliding
> Down through the turning sphere
> His ready harbinger,
>   With turtle wing the amorous clouds dividing,
> And waving wide her myrtle wand,
> She strikes a universal peace through sea and land.
>
> (45–52)

It is the epithet 'amorous' which finally kills it. In another context that
'softly sliding' might have been beautiful. Here it suggests a well-
oiled mechanism in a masque by Inigo Jones. It is interesting to note
that the first lines of *The Passion* (which are *about* the Nativity
Ode) describe it in terms of a theatrical spectacle. Later the poem
(119 f.) Milton alludes to Job, xxxviii.7: '. . . When the morning stars
sang together, and all the sons of God shouted for joy', but his humanism cannot swallow that 'shouted for joy' and so he suppresses it.
Stanza xiv is another good example of this barren marriage between
humanism and Christian tradition.

   Yet there is in the poem one marvellous, extended passage, that
which tells how the birth of Christ causes all the dark pagan gods, the
lemures, mooned Ashtaroth, wounded Thammuz, sullen Moloch,
the grisly king, the brutish gods of Nile, to withdraw from the
world. Milton makes brilliant use of his learning in choosing wherever
possible a barbaric variant on a classical name; thus Jupiter becomes
the African Hammon, Adonis the Phoenician Thammuz. This is the

obscure and bloody region which Frazer, in a spirit of rationalism, explored in *The Golden Bough*. It has become commonplace to observe that Frazer's work was not received in the spirit in which it was offered. The poets and writers of the twentieth century, instead of finding in *The Golden Bough* a comparative analysis of barbaric religion, felt they were exploring their own inmost beliefs. T. S. Eliot in the 1920s could react to this murky and violent world with something approaching nostalgia. The religious preoccupation of *The Waste Land* is remarkably promiscuous. Milton's attitude is, to put it mildly, different.

So here we have a wonderful idea: the incarnation of Christ viewed, so to speak, spatially, as gradually irradiating the world, hunting from their lairs all misshapen creatures of the spirit. But the idea suffers from the way in which it is joined to the main body of the poem. Milton opens this section on the expulsion of the pagan gods by telling how Christ has bound 'the old dragon underground' (168). The 'old dragon' is the Serpent, that is, Satan himself. He moves from this without break to list the pagan gods. Now these, it is clear, are not intended to have a literal status. Rather they are a figurative means of describing the withering away of idolatry. Similarly, when Nietzsche said 'God is dead', he did not mean that a real spiritual individual had perished; he meant that religion was finished. But Milton draws no dividing line between the dragon and the dumb oracles. The suggestion is that the two are co-ordinate. The effect of this is, as with the Baroque nature-sequence, to weaken the supernatural element of the poem. If Anubis is a metaphor for idolatry, we ask, half-consciously, then why should not the dragon be a metaphor for wickedness, and 'the infant God' a metaphor for righteousness? There is only one way to cure this, and that is to make it clear that Thammuz, Osiris and the rest are real devils, working under the dragon. This is what Milton did in his reworking of the idea in Book I of *Paradise Lost* (365 ff.). But in the Nativity Ode, Christ is in real danger of assimilation to the level of mythological fable.

My account of the Nativity Ode may have erred on the side of hostility. It may further be charged with inconsistency, since it seems that the things for which I blame it—its rejection of immediacy and warmth—are the very things for which earlier I praised Milton. But we are now in a position to answer such a charge at once. In the first part of this introduction I argued that Milton's austerities of diction were valuable when they resulted in authoritative and intelligible poetic structures, analogous to the great poses of Renaissance painting. In the Nativity Ode no such result is achieved. We find in it neither the imaginative impetus nor the discipline of *Comus*, much less of *Paradise Lost*. As it is, the effect is diffuse and incoherent. The piecemeal application of humanist gew-gaws to Elizabethan versification is not at all the same thing as what Milton later achieved, that is the creation of an heroic language through the sustained tension of native and alien structures. And it is certainly no adequate disguise for deficiencies in religious insight.

V

The Elizabethans liked versified debates, consisting of thesis and antithesis. Normally the points of view were argued by different poets. For example a pair of poems closely related to *L'Allegro* and *Il Penseroso* was written by Fletcher and Strode. That *L'Allegro* and *Il Penseroso* were written by one man emphasizes the high degree of artifice, though it may be that Milton, by giving the last word to the meditative man, intended the second view not just to balance but also to cancel the first, and so was presenting, dramatically, a real opinion. Milton was not short of opinions; and it is characteristic of his genius to conclude his debates with a narrowly won but genuine resolution. But we must not burden these poems with the wrong sort of seriousness. They are related also to the light-hearted academic exercises in rhetorical 'proof' which were in vogue at Cambridge in Milton's time. These were competitions in felicitous ingenuity rather than in logical demonstration. Their atmosphere must have been closer to the school debating society than the law court. Milton is here in his Shakespearean dress, and thinking more perhaps of *A Midsummer Night's Dream* than of any other play. At times one is forced to acknowledge that he has, as the eighteenth-century editors used to say, 'improved upon his author'. Shakespeare's

> And then the whole quire hold their hips and laugh
> (*A Midsummer Night's Dream*, II.i.55)

becomes in Milton:

> Laughter holding both his sides

The nature of the change is interesting. First Milton has pulled the line together, made it terser. Secondly he has detached it from its specific, narrative function and turned it into a generic figure, mere Laughter with a capital L. In fact, the poems show very clearly how Milton could, at a pinch, achieve an effect of decorum without transgressing the limits of the vernacular. One might have thought that Milton could have achieved his austerity of diction only by a firm adherence to classical forms of speech, since only then could he make it clear that he was deliberately renouncing ordinary language. Yet, somehow, in a line which is ostentatiously Saxon, we get the same impression of choice and exclusion:

> Quips and cranks and wanton wiles

I have said 'ostentatiously Saxon' and perhaps this is the clue. The words are so rugged, so *consistently* unpolished, that one feels they cannot be there by accident. What Spenser could not do, Milton, in some measure, could.

   Milton, it seems, is not averse to puzzling his reader a little. He likes the word which seems low, or incongrous, but which the reader is finally forced to concede as correct. He is more faithful to Aristotle's opinion that an unusual word can heighten the effect of a line (*Poetics*, 1458a) than to Caesar's 'Flee the unusual word as sailors flee submerged rocks'.[1] This delight in extorting assent from the learned reader shows clearly in such phrases as 'Jonson's learned sock' (*L'Allegro*, 132). This is perhaps funnier now than it was in the seventeenth century, but it must always have sounded distinctly odd. Dryden's similar line:

> Nor greater Jonson dares in socks appear
> (*Mac Flecknoe*, 80)

is much less ostentatiously opposed to English idiom. The allusion is to the comic actor's slipper, for which the Latin is *soccus*, as in Horace, *Ars Poetica*, 80.

> hunc socci cepere pedem grandesque cothurni.[2]

Thus unnatural English is justified by being made the echo of accepted Latin usage. Such freaks of learning often lie buried beneath even the most natural and innocent-sounding English. Confronted with a phrase like 'The cynosure of neighbouring eyes', every schoolboy realises that he must look up the notes. But how many even pause on the phrase 'jolly hours' in the sonnet on the nightingale? In fact, 'jolly hours' is a phrase of Homer and lies there as a tiny prize for the humanist reader. 'Decent shoulders' (*Il Penseroso*, 36) similarly reflects the Latin use of *decens* to mean 'beautifying' or just 'beautiful' (as in Horace, *Odes*, III.xxvii.53). *On Time* contains (at line 18) the almost childish phrase 'happy-making sight' and it is only the occasional reader who notices that if one translates 'beatific vision' into Latin and then back into Saxon English one arrives at Milton's phrase. It might be supposed that Milton is here striving, like William Morris or Gerard Manley Hopkins, to impart freshness and concrete vigour by transposing from the borrowed word to the Saxon equivalent, but surely this is the opposite of the truth. When Milton wrote, the

---

[1] Remark recorded by Aulus Gellius *Attic Nights* I.x.4

[2] 'This metre was adopted by both the comic sock and high tragic buskin'.
Cf. Horace *Epistles* II.i.174, *Satires* I.v.64.

phrase 'beatific vision' was a very recent import into the language.
There can have been no sense of an exhausted idiom which needed to
be revived. Milton seldom wants us to pass insensibly through his
description to the thing itself. He prefers to delay us *en route*, to divert
part of our attention to the linguistic medium itself. This is what it
means when we say that Milton writes not a transparent but an opaque
style. Thus, in a phrase like 'happy-making sight' he *wants* us to hesi-
tate over the linguistic authority of the idiom. Although his language
is ostensibly simple his intention is devious. He is creating the very
abstractness of language which Hopkins was later to attack.

Such minor tricks of style are seldom anything but slight irritants.
But they are symptomatic of something larger and more valuable.
This strange hybrid language, this horny membrane which Milton
interposes between the reader and the subject is itself a work of high
abstract art. If it were a total barrier between the reader and any sort
of reality we should be forced, ultimately, to deplore its creation.
As things are, it is productive primarily of tension. Meaning and image
are accessible to the reader but only after a certain effort. Of course,
in *L'Allegro* and *Il Penseroso* all this is only beginning to be true.
Nevertheless all the distinctively Miltonic features of these poems
point towards tension and away from cool harmony. And this
again suggests that within the context of our comparison of Milton
with the great painters of the Italian Renaissance he must be placed
nearer to the restless Michelangelo than to the tranquil Raphael.

VI

Milton was now ready to stretch his powers a little further. The
greater part of Shakespeare's development takes place within a single
form—drama. All his profound modifications are thus in a sense
internal. But every stage of Milton's development finds instantaneous
outward expression in a change of vehicle. His development is
formally graduated: from lyric to masque, from masque to epic. So

here, as he begins to write *Comus*, we may think of him as moving into his second phase. There is a little hesitation, a brief try-out of the form with *Arcades*, and then the full-scale achievement of *Comus* itself.

Masque is essentially esoteric. It is an 'in-form' designed to be acted and watched by people who know one another well. Any boy who has been to a play acted by his schoolfellows will know that one of the keenest pleasures of the occasion consists in recognising e.g. one's old friend Bloggs as e.g. Polonius. Of course, this pleasure is illicit. Polonius is a character in *Hamlet*, a play written for professional actors. Thus you are not supposed to think about Bloggs as Bloggs, but only about Bloggs as Polonius. But masque is a form in which this pleasure of personal recognition is not illicit but authorised. Naturally, when the playwright never intended us to recognise our friends in costume, any such recognition, when it occurs, will be incongruous and so will tend to make us laugh. But in masque there is no such discordancy but rather a carefully framed congruity.

Comus was written to adorn, and also in a way poetically to explore a specific occasion, the election of the Earl of Bridgewater as Lord President of Wales. It was an occasion of serious festivity. Milton's masque tells the story of a young lady's chaste triumph over baser nature. The parts of the lady and her brothers were taken by the Earl's children, Alice, the Lord Brackley and Thomas. It is no accident that Chastity was not only represented in the story but also actually acted by a young girl. The careful mirroring of nature whereby brother took the part of brother was also deliberate. At the end of the masque, image magically dissolves into reality and the scene presents 'Ludlow Town and the President's Castle'—that is, the very place where the children were in fact performing. Sometimes, in shops or public exhibitions, one sees a television screen showing people entering the very room in which it is placed. People glancing at the screen thus get a glimpse of themselves through the eyes of a third person. The experience is oddly disturbing, and provides a better analogy to the elaborately metaphorical structure of masque than a mirror, with its simple, frontal reflection. The Spirit, at this point still within the story, presents the children to their mother and father, in a dance of ceremonious innocence. Up to this point the Earl and his wife have been, technically, spectators of the play. Now the glittering enchanted figures of the masque, dance forward to draw them into the circle of light created by Milton.

It is thus part of the tradition of masque to act out the real situation in mythological terms.[1] Things become more complex still when masque is made the poetic vehicle of a Platonist metaphysic. The sense that a chaste girl does not merely exemplify an abstraction, chastity, but also incarnates or even resembles an ideal spiritual essence, Chastity with a capital C, permeates *Comus*. The notion of the spiritual and the ideal interpenetrating the corrupt and earthy world below the moon is a sort of echo of that other interpenetration, of art and reality, already described.

The antithesis between the spiritual and the corrupt is conveyed by metaphors of light and darkness, yet even here, if we are to be accurate, we must acknowledge a blurring or interpenetration of categories. The belief that the light-filled regions above the moon were incorruptible and nearer to the angels could still be seriously asserted in 1634. Thus the evaluative language, moving between the starry heavens and 'the smoke and stir of this dim spot' itself trembles between metaphorical and literal.

The argument of the poem—the defeat of Comus, or Revel—is ascetic. But it would be a mistake to see it in the twentieth-century terms of a conflict between virtue and happiness. Since utilitarianism, with its doctrine of 'the greatest happiness of the greatest number,' it has been unusual to draw any strong distinction between happiness and pleasure. But for Milton happiness is a more objective conception than it is for us, and comprises both our 'better off' and

---

[1] For examples of this, see Rosemond Tuve *Images and Themes in Five Poems by Milton* Cambridge, Mass., 1957 pp. 117f.; also E. K. Chambers *The Elizabethan Stage* Oxford, 1923, I pp. 144, 151.

'blessed'. For him the divine discontent of Socrates is certainly a happier state than the contentment of a well-fed pig. And indeed even in these post-utilitarian times most of us can understand how the former condition, though less pleasurable, is more enviable. Milton's philosophy is made clear by the Attendant Spirit's description of Comus's victims, their features transformed into a bestial shape:

> And they, so perfect is their misery,
> Not once perceive their foul disfigurement,
> But boast themselves more comely than before . . .
>   (73–5)

The logic of utilitarianism is exactly reversed. The very feature which for Bentham would have safeguarded their happiness—that is, their ignorance—is for Milton the chief element in the 'misery', or objective spiritual humiliation. The Lady is happier than Comus.

A similar modern error would be to view the conflict of the masque as a struggle between the moral and the aesthetic. But 'the sunclad power of chastity' is not merely a more blessed condition than depravity, it is also more beautiful. In aesthetic terms the distinction we are offered is that between the truly and the falsely beautiful. Comus himself is given (at some risk to the proper psychological simplicity of masque) a wonderful speech describing his reaction to the Lady's Song:

> But such a sacred, and home-felt delight,
> Such sober certainty of waking bliss
> I never heard till now.
>   (262–4)

In the opinion of Comus, and, since it is Comus's better self who speaks, in the opinion of Milton also, it is no part of the intention of this poem that the devil should have all the good tunes. But here we encounter a difficulty. For many readers have wished to dissent from Comus's critical judgment. They find him too modest; his own poetry is, they feel, superior to anything which comes in this poem from the lips of Virtue.

The roots of this disagreement go deep. Broadbent, writing on the Nativity Ode, called it a 'Miltonic victory . . . a schematic conquest'.[1] It is curious how Milton's struggles in the process of composition find symbolic expression in the resultant poem. The struggle between Comus and the Lady is among other things the stylistic struggle of Milton's life, and the long war between the native and the classical tradition. More precisely, it appears in *Comus* as a struggle between the idiom of Greek drama and that of English.

VII

The language of Greek drama is, to put it mildly, odd. Anyone who wishes to find out more about this should consult A. E. Housman's brilliant and only partially unfair parody. Dwight MacDonald has called this parody a burlesque of 'the horrors of classical translation, mitigated of late years by the noble work of Dudley Fitts, Robert Fitzgerald and Richmond Lattimore'.[2] But in fact Housman is parodying Greek tragedy itself. The weird antitheses, the harsh exigencies of line by line dialogue (technically 'stichomythia') whereby a speaker must always be interrupted if he has more than a line's worth to say, the outlandish metaphors—are all present in the text of Greek tragedy and are less obvious in the work of Dudley Fitts etc. than in Sir Richard Jebb only because they are less literal than he. Housman's parody is a mosaic of quotations.

Now it is an interesting thing that those very oddities of expression which Housman parodied and the modern translator suppresses seem actually to have attracted Milton. There is no closer analogy

---

[1] 'The Nativity Ode' in *The Living Milton* ed. F. Kermode, London, 1960 p. 27
[2] Note appended to the text of Housman's parody in *Parodies* ed. D. Mac-Donald, London, 1960 p. 318.

(outside Greek tragedy itself) to the stichomythia of Housman than
the stichomythia of *Comus* 277–89. It appears then (and the inference
is supported by his superbly literal version of Horace, Odes, 1.v)
that Milton is working with a wholly different concept of translation from that now fashionable. Where the modern translator feels
that he has not fully rendered his author into English if he has
failed to smooth out those linguistic oddities which are peculiar to
the original language, Milton plainly thought that such total
naturalisation of an author could be achieved only by dropping
everything most urgently needed by the English language. The
Penguin translator of Æschylus can be said to have done a good
job by modern standards in that what he gives us is certainly English.
Milton was willing to write lines like:

> But who are these? for with joint pace I hear
> The tread of many feet steering this way. . . .[1]
> (*Samson Agonistes*, 110–11)

which is not certainly English but perhaps tells us more about Æschylus. Note also that Milton's lines, though 'unnatural', are intelligible.
The minimum duty of clarification is faithfully discharged. One
might compare the translator with a man who is asked to carry a
large awkwardly-shaped burden through a narrow gate into his
native city. The modern man, Procrustes-like, lops off the corners and
passes easily through the gate. Milton, on the contrary, carries his
burden as though it were sacred, and after great strain and some dam-
age to the gate-posts gets it within his city walls. Of course, different
sorts of translation are necessary for different purposes. But anyone
who has had the experience of growing irritated with a smooth
modern translation, and of longing for some really primitive, literal
crib in order to get a notion of the way an ancient poem was actually

---

[1] Compare Housman's parody:
  Chorus: Sailing on horseback, or with feet for oars?
  Alc.: Plying with speed my partnership of legs . . .

put together—may begin to think that Milton is not so much our greatest as our only translator. Of course one reason for the difference in method between Milton and the modern lies in the attitude to the English language. The modern assumes that English is a rich and sufficient idiom. Milton assumed that it was in part impoverished, in part exhausted. Ironically, it is the Miltonic readiness to adopt alien idioms which has gradually made the English language so rich and flexible as almost to justify the unreceptive attitude of the moderns. In the days when the Latin for 'remorse of conscience' had to be translated 'the again-bite of inwit', things were different.

In fact it is curious how the greater poets, responding to ancient literature, tend to follow a method very similar to that of the schoolboy's shilling crib, that is to wrench into English not only such translatable things as images but also such untranslatable things as idioms. Ben Jonson translated Horace *Odes* IV, i. 1–3:

> Intermissa, Venus, diu
>   rursus bella moves? parce, precor, precor.

as follows:

> Venus, again thou mov'st a war
>   Long intermitted; pray thee, pray thee spare . . . [1]

The translator of the Penguin Horace, James Michie, has

> Must it be war again
>   After so long a truce? Venus, be kind, refrain.

Michie's rendering is more pointed, and indeed more attractive than Jonson's. Yet in the long run the less accessible excellence of Jonson is the more satisfying. Certainly it is Jonson who is dragging up the English language by its hair. In Milton's own translation of Horace

---

[1] Jonson's translation is printed alongside the Latin text in *The Odes of Horace* ed. H. E. Butler, London, 1929 pp. 243–5.

> qui nunc te fruitur credulus aurea

appears in English, word for word, as

> who now enjoys thee credulous, all gold.

which, though barely intelligible without the Latin, is yet so much better than Michie's lucid

> He's still credulous, though, hugging the prize he thinks
> Pure gold. . . .

Dryden's practice in translation is occasionally similar. But perhaps a closer analogy to Milton, because concerned with a general heightening of English rather than with the rendering of a single, complete text, is T. S. Eliot:

> What seas what shores what grey rocks and what islands
> What water lapping the bow . . . [1]

The immediate source of this is Seneca, imitating Greek tragedy. But Eliot with his string of unpunctuated interrogative pronouns has stepped across his author Seneca to Seneca's own Greek author. The idiom is not natural to English but good poetry can afford to swallow such idioms; in a way it can scarcely afford not to.

In *Comus* the Greek idioms are given to the Lady, while the English, that is the Shakespearean, the Jonsonian, *etc.*, are given to Comus. The contrast between the two is harshly asserted in the dialogue:

> *Lady* To find out that, good shepherd, I suppose
> In such a scant allowance of star-light,
> Would overtask the best land-pilot's art,
> Without the sure guess of well-practis'd feet.

---

[1] The opening lines of *Marina*. Cf. Housman's parody:
> . . . wherefore seeking whom
> Whence by what way how purposed art thou come . . . ?

Comus I know each lane, and every alley green
            Dingle, or bushy dell of this wide wood . . .
                                                    (307–12)

Critics who sense something *voulu*, some conscious exercise of the will in the Lady's speech in contrast with something spontaneous, natural and sensuous in Comus's are surely right; but that does not necessarily make them right to prefer the language of Comus. In Freudian terms (and they are relevant to Milton's poem) Comus speaks the language of the Id, the Lady language of the Ego. It comes naturally to the post-Freudian critic to prefer the former. Milton, to whom virtue was very much a matter of the will, would see the stylistic collision as echoing the moral.

Since Nietzsche wrote his celebrated essay on tragedy it has become common to think of artists as involved necessarily with the Dionysiac principle, that is with the impulsive, the irrational, the intoxicating. It needs no great labour to show that Comus is a Dionysiac figure. Milton himself tells us his parentage. But Dionysus, revered by the twentieth century, is regarded by Milton as a daemon, almost a devil. Our own century is pre-occupied with the aesthetic of release. Milton was interested in the aesthetic of inhibition. This shadowy, beautiful, libidinous figure is carefully chosen by Milton as the victim of a righteous conquest.

Here again the moral struggle is strangely mingled with what might appear to be a merely literary enterprise. Festive masque, like Elizabethan festive comedy, is connected with holiday ritual, and as such celebrates riot, misrule and merriment. Dionysus, Bacchus, the Spring Lord, Robin, the May King, Comus, are all different aspects of the same being. But Milton's masque celebrates, not Comus, but Chastity. It is sometimes forgotten that Milton took up the ancient form of epic in *Paradise Lost* not only for docile imitation, but also to correct its unregenerate morality. Similarly, he enters the world of masque in order to depose its ancient king.

Thus Milton's poem is about the defeat of wantonness by virtue, the defeat of English idiom by Greek, and ultimately the defeat of masque itself. It is a profound and, in a way, heroic idea, even if not wholly sympathetic. But it remains doubtful whether Milton entirely brought it off.

VIII

First of all it is essential to Milton's idea that reason should be, and be seen to be, on the Lady's side. But the doctrine of chastity offered in the masque is more magical than rational. The first exposition of the subject occurs in the brothers' debate, lines 350–480. It may be that the static nature of this dialogue is justified by its occurring in a masque, and not a drama. It is, however, not merely static but also frivolous. Anyone who makes the experiment of taking the elder brother seriously will see at once that what he says is simply false.[1] A girl is not rendered invulnerable by chastity. The force of this objection would surely be perfectly clear to a seventeenth-century man. In Shakespeare's *Richard II* a similarly magical doctrine of royal invulnerability is put into the mouth of the king:

> For every man that Bolinbroke hath press'd
> To lift shrewd steel against our golden crown,
> God for his Richard hath in heavenly pay
> A glorious angel . . .
>
> (III.ii.58–62)

But the rest of *Richard II* (unlike *Comus*) is all about King Richard's defeat and deposition at the hands of Bolingbroke. Of course in *Comus* one cannot deny the presence of considerable poetic power in the brothers' language. But it is the wrong kind of power. It is in fact verbal sorcery, nearer to the arts of Comus than to the sage

[1] It might be objected that the whole speech is allegorical; and means that Chastity will, *sub specie aeternitatis*, prevail over Lasciviousness. This would certainly save the speech from my strictures, but seems to me a strained interpretation in view of the context.

doctrine which is required. The Elder Brother's allusions to Plato's *Phaedo* (e.g. 470–5) fail to supply the defect of plain reason. The *Phaedo* is as it happens a strange interweaving of rational and super-stitious elements, and Milton has chosen to borrow one of the superstitions. The Second Brother's comment, line 476, 'How charming is divine philosophy!' (where 'charming' means 'spell-binding') is only too accurate.

The second theoretic refutation of Comus is conducted by the Lady herself, lines 756–99. She is a good deal better than her brothers. She meets Comus's praise of excess with an argument I am willing to respect, namely that if all received fair shares the overwhelming abundance described by Comus would cease forthwith. This is a simple economic thesis, and it is to the point. No economist appeared to argue Comus's case until 1703, when Bernard de Mandeville claimed that the excesses of the rich were essential to the economic well-being of the many. But the trouble with the Lady's speech is that it does not go far enough. She tackles Comus at the economic level, but the real heart of the matter, 'the sage and serious doctrine of virginity' remains unexpounded.

There are signs in the textual history of *Comus* that Milton was worried about this very point. In 1637 he added lines 779–806 in which the Lady says that she could argue the case for chastity but that Comus would not be able to understand her if she did. This seems at best an incomplete solution. Of course, the bald summary I have just given grotesquely diminishes the power of the original speech. But it does not distort its logic. When we ask, 'What are the sources of this power?' we shall arrive at the same answer we reached with the dialogue of the brothers. The Lady's speech *tells* us that virginity is not only a 'high mystery' but also a 'serious doctrine' (i.e., it has a logical structure) but does not *show* us. The telling is superb—'the sun-clad power of Chastity' (782) is, as a mere phrase, almost irresist-able. In fact the Lady's imperious words are a mixture of bullying and enchantment. Comus is not matched save by his own arts. Here is her conclusion (which makes Comus shudder with fear):

> ... the uncontrolled worth
> Of this pure cause would kindle my rapt spirits
> To such a flame of sacred vehemence,
> That dumb things would be mov'd to sympathise,
> And the brute earth would lend her nerves, and shake,
> Till all thy magic structures rear'd so high,
> Were shatter'd into heaps o'er thy false head.
>   (793–9)

This is, of course, marvellous, but is it marvellous in the right way?
It is hardly the 'sober certainty of waking bliss' that Comus found in
her song. Of course she is now struggling with the enemy, but she
should not therefore cease to be herself. Technically, these lines are
hyperbole. It is questionable whether such a figure of speech should
have occurred in the Lady's lines at all. When Truth is struggling
with false Indulgence, she ought not to exaggerate. One simply is
not able to believe the claim she makes. It smacks too much of Pros-
pero taming the elements, too much, in short, of the magician.
Comus is driven back, not by 'home-felt' truth but by a stronger
magic than his own. His phrase, 'some superior power', like the
Second Brother's, line 476, is sufficiently accurate.

It follows from my analysis of the Lady's speech that I can have no
objection to Comus's fantastic and wonderful hyperbole, lines 732–6:

> ... th'unsought diamonds
> Would so emblaze the forehead of the deep
> And so bestud with stars that they below
> Would grow inur'd to light, and come at last
> To gaze upon the sun with shameless brows.

This magnificent debauchery of language, in the mouth of Comus, is
absolutely right.

It may be that the intermingling of superstitions and rational elements in what ought to be the realm of Christian truth is a symptom
of a wider uncertainty in *Comus*. The character Comus is, in part, the
Spirit of the Wood, the trackless place outside the walls of the Chris-

tian polity, the place of strange pagan survivals, brute violence, absence of 'civility' in the old sense. I have already alluded to the connexion: Comus-Revel-Masque-May King-Misrule. But when Milton comes to treat this world of rustic superstition his Puritan resolution falters. His case was probably not unique. In the 1580s the Puritan Philip Stubbes had described the May rites as follows:

> But the chiefest jewel they bring from thence is their Maypole, which they bring home with great veneration, as thus: They have twenty or forty yoke of oxen, every oxe having a sweet nose-gay of flowers placed on the tip of his horns, and these oxen draw home this Maypole (this stinking idol, rather) which is covered all over with flowers and herbs, bound round about with strings, from the top to the bottom, and sometime painted with variable colours, with two or three hundred men, women and children following it with great devotion. And thus being reared up with handkerchiefs and flags hovering on the top, they strew the ground round about, bind green boughs about it, set up summer halls, bowers and arbours hard by it. And then fall they to dance about it like as the heathen people did at the dedication of the Idols, whereof this is a perfect pattern, or rather the thing itself. I have heard it credibly reported (and that *viva voce*) by men of great gravity and reputation, that of forty, three-score, or a hundred maids going to the wood, there have scarcely the third part of them returned home again undefiled. These be the fruits which these cursed pastimes bring forth.[1]

The remarkable thing about this description is its complete opposition of image and concept. Stubbes succeeds better than any author I have read at conveying the beauty of the old May festivals. In such a context of loving description the strictly judicial phrases, like 'this stinking idol, rather' are experienced as dislocation.

---

[1] *The Anatomie of Abuses* (1583) ed. F. J. Furnivall, London, 1877–82 Part I, p. 149.

At a more sophisticated level, *Comus* is ambiguous in a very similar way. Allusions to rustic festivals recur and seem closely involved with its theme. Because *Comus* is a masque, it was written for a specific occasion and even for a specific place. The occasion is the appointment of a great governing, civilising figure, the Lord President of Wales. The place is Ludlow and the Welsh Marches. It is worth remembering that in Milton's time the contrast between the far west of England, with its huge forests, and imperfectly civilised inhabitants on the one hand and on the other the profoundly ordered and civilised eastern half of the country was marked. Even today it is perceptible. It is probable that the Lady's sovereignty over Comus was, if only half-consciously, felt to symbolise the Earl of Bridgewater's sovereignty over his wild territory. Of course the echoes of this symbolism extend indefinitely, even to embrace such general notions as the triumph of Christianity over paganism. Given this basic structure, one might have expected from Milton a judicial condemnation of ancient rituals in so far as they were not clearly Christian. For a while, indeed, we seem to be offered this. At line 171 the Lady seems to show real horror at the thought that she may encounter some such festival:

> ... methought it was the sound
> Of riot and ill-manag'd merriment,
> Such as the jocund flute or gamesome pipe
> Stirs up among the loose unletter'd hinds,
> When for their teeming flocks, and granges full,
> In wanton dance they praise the bounteous Pan
> And thank the gods amiss. I should be loth
> To meet the rudeness and swill'd insolence
> Of such late wassailers. ...

The tone is not entirely certain. One wonders for a moment whether the Lady is taking a kindly view of the worship of Pan as a sort of lisping Christianity.

But by the time the paragraph is completed the general pejorative character is clear enough. Yet near the end of the masque the restoration of the Lady to her father is celebrated by just such a festive ritual as was earlier condemned. The pagan character of this country dance is even asserted by the poet, lines 962–5:

> . . . such court guise
> As Mercury did first devise
> With the mincing Dryades
> On the lawns, and on the leas.

By an irony which transfixes the very heart of the poem, Milton found that the only world his poem would accept as the proper environment for innocence was the pre-Christian world which his own Puritan ego had rejected as sunk in sin. One senses that, in a way, Comus has won after all. This sequence implicitly acknowledges the holiday truth of Comus's

> Beauty is nature's brag, and must be shown
> In courts, at feasts, on high solemnities. . . .
>
> (745–6)

When the Attendant Spirit describes the nymph Sabrina who is to liberate the Lady from her magic bondage, he seems to be echoing Comus's earlier description of the goddess of the woods. Here is the Attendant Spirit:

> . . . oft at eve
> Visits the herds along the twilight meadows,
> Helping all urchin blasts, and ill luck signs
> That the shrewd meddling elf delights to make,
> Which she with precious vial'd liquors heals.
> For which the shepherds at their festivals
> Carol her goodness loud in rustic lays,
> And throw sweet garland wreaths into her stream
> Of pansies, pinks and gaudy daffodils.
>
> (843–51)

And here is Comus:

> . . . the goddess that in rural shrine
> Dwell'st here with Pan or Sylvan, by blest song
> Forbidding every bleak unkindly fog
> To touch the prosperous growth of this tall wood.
>
> (267–70)

Again (the pattern is growing familiar) Comus the nature spirit is defeated not by Grace, or Reason, but by another nature spirit. It is interesting that the Lady's part in the drama remains, despite Milton's efforts to redeem the situation by infusions of superb poetry, negative. She does not act; she is only acted upon. Despite the Elder Brother's elaborate panegyric, she can do nothing of her own accord.

IX

Between 1634 and 1637 Milton wrote almost no poetry. He assiduously revised *Comus*, and wrote a couple of minor lyrics. Then comes a sudden access of energy and the superb *At a Solemn Music*. It was immediately followed by *Lycidas*, which can be called, without absurdity, the best lyric poem in the English language. It is interesting to ask in connexion with *Lycidas* a question which was more fashionable two hundred years ago than it is today: what, if any, are its artistic defects? The principal weak point, surely, is the speech of Peter. John Crowe Ransom claimed that he 'sounds like another Puritan zealot, and less than apostolic'. There is a real want of tact in using Peter as a political mouthpiece, even where (or perhaps especially where) the politics are ecclesiastical. There is a place in the *Divine Comedy*[1] where Dante describes himself as being put through an examination by St Peter and passing with honours. The two passages are bad in a very similar way. It at once becomes clear what is

[1] *Paradiso* xxiv. 46–154.

wrong if we imagine Thomas Aquinas reading them, or better still God. They are, in a Christian context, presumptuous.

The second fault comes at the end of the poem (before the coda) where we are told that Lycidas will become a sort of *genius loci*, or spirit of the shore. What is strange here is the relapse into paganism (in some ways analogous to the relapse in *Comus*). It may be said that I fail to appreciate the nature of pastoral, the fact that Christian truths are shadowed beneath a traditional and pagan veil. But this is not true of *Lycidas*. Hitherto in the poem the Christian elements have been allowed to transcend the pastoral convention. At one point, of course, they intersect. The shepherd is a cardinal image of the Gospels as it is of pastoral. But the 'pilot of the Galilean lake'(109), 'the dear might of him that walk'd the waves' (173), 'the saints above' (178)—these phrases shake themselves free from the pastoral disguise. After such a preparation there is a serious incongruity in snatching Lycidas from Heaven and confining him to Earth.

But when this is said I believe the case against *Lycidas* is complete. And of these two charges the second must be qualified. The transition to the 'Genius of the shore' is musically supremely beautiful. We have passed the climax of the poem, and Milton modulates his tone, before the distancing coda, 'Thus sang the uncouth swain', where the diction is light, the sense of 'mere pastoral' suddenly strong again.

A similar effect can be secured on the stage by quenching the lights behind a gauze curtain and then illuminating the curtain itself. The ancient sublimities of incarnation and resurrection which had blazed through the pastoral film now grow dim again, and we are left with the same sunlight stealing from the hills, the shepherd with his pipe. Some have objected to the trivial and tortuous pastoral allegory in which Milton recalls his time as an undergraduate at Cambridge (25–36). I personally find it more poignant every time I read it, and when Dr Johnson quotes it in ridicule my only impulse is to put away Johnson and re-read *Lycidas*. But it is not easy to demonstrate its merit in a way that would convince a sceptic. This indeed is a characteristic of the poem as a whole. *Lycidas* is, in a special sense, 'pure poetry'. I do not mean by this that it is necessarily good poetry. In the sense in which I use the word, *King Lear* is less pure than *Lycidas*, yet I believe *King Lear* to be better. By 'pure poetry' I mean that poetry which is most resistant to paraphrase, which, in the words of Robert Frost, 'gets lost in translation'.

Certain of the concepts worked out in this introduction can be applied to *Lycidas*. For example, in the Nativity Ode and in *Comus* I have suggested a strange infusion of Milton's difficulties in *writing* into the subject matter of the poem. The first lines of *Lycidas* are a further example of this. The reader is invited to look and work it out for himself. Again, examples of Milton's ability to assimilate the most obstinately Saxon words to the canons of stern decorum can be seen in 'welter' at 13, 'hairy' at 104 and 'oozy' at 175. Many a poet who feels far less 'classical' than Milton would have shrunk from using such 'un-classical' words. The distinctively Miltonic blending of audacity and high literary discipline can be seen in such expressions as 'melodious tear' (14). The phrase 'somewhat loudly' (17) repels many readers at first encounter, but conceals a strange power. Milton, so bookish, seemingly so far removed from the spoken voice, here catches perfectly the deliberate pause of the practised minstrel as he secures the attention of his listeners.

Is the whole poem, then, a merely technical feat? This is essentially the position of Northrop Frye though he would quarrel with the word 'merely'. For him, the poem has no subject in the real world. It deals not with a person, but with an archetype, Orpheus-Christ-Adonis, the dying god or daemon; Milton is concerned, before all else, with the convention of elegy, with lamentation over extinguished beauty. Frye writes:

> . . . Milton was deeply interested in the structure and symbolism of funeral elegies, and had been practising since adolescence on every fresh corpse in sight, from the university beadle to the fair infant dying of a cough.[1]

[1] In *Lycidas: the Tradition and the Poem* ed. Patrides p. 206

This is witty, but in a way Frye's wit has betrayed his argument. It lets out the fact that each of Milton's exercises in elegy is in fact attached to a real person, an actual event. Theocritus, in his first idyll, felt no such obligation to confine himself to a real death. Thus the interesting thing is Milton's admittedly minimal but nevertheless conscientious adherence to the rule of truth. Frye's archetypal account of *Lycidas* involves a flattening out of the poem's pointed, objective reference. In fact, as M. H. Abrams observed,[1] *Lycidas* is about Edward King and Christ. Orpheus enters as a secondary image only.

But the aspect of reality with which Milton is most profoundly concerned is, of course, himself. The sense of Milton's own career, ambitions, pride, is so strong in the poem as to revive the force of Johnson's complaint that Milton's grief for King is insufficient. The usual answer to Johnson is that his approach is naively literal. But if Milton is a literal presence in the poem, why cannot King be? The sense that Milton cares more about Milton than about his drowned friend is in fact very strong. Our primary impression is of a strong excitement; the moment has come for Milton to lift his voice again, to perform a new feat of poetry. The excitement predominates over the grief. It may well be better for the writing that this is so. In Matthew Arnold's *Thyrsis*, where the grief plainly predominates over the egotistical excitement, the effect is sadly inferior. Milton's ambition is as important in *Lycidas* as it is in his nineteenth sonnet. When we read that fame is the 'last infirmity of noble mind' we may suppose for a moment that Milton is 'seeing through' literary aspiration. But then comes Phoebus's reply: the approbation of Jove himself is a legitimate object of ambition. Thus what we took for scepticism concerning the desire for glory as such turns out to be only a doubt about the value of a changeable and ill-founded reputation; the trouble with most writers is not that they are over-ambitious but that they are too easily satisfied with perishable rewards. The

---

[1] In *Lycidas: the Tradition and the Poem* ed. Patrides p. 226.

nature of Milton's attitude is neatly shown by his transformation of a Virgilian motif at line 77:

Phoebus repli'd, and touch'd my trembling ears . . .

This line has, in my opinion, been misunderstood. The touching of the ears echoes a passage in Virgil (*Eclogues*, vi. 3–5) where a god rebukes the poet for attempting epic themes when he should stick to pastoral. The line in *Lycidas* is therefore explained as showing divine disapproval of excessive ambition. But the context makes it clear that Milton has in fact reversed the Virgilian idea. Apollo rebukes the poet for setting his sights too low.

X

After *Lycidas* we descend, but not disastrously. Milton's sonnets, written at a time when the golden age of Elizabethan sonneteering had burned itself out, are in their harsh honesty, their refusal to intoxicate, strangely heroic. The linguistic basis of this achievement has been explained by F. T. Prince, in his *The Italian Element in Milton's Verse* (1954). In essence, it consists in a new relation with antiquity.[1] Milton's classicism is not a matter of vocabulary, but of syntax, of sentence-structure. Word by word, the sonnet on the Piedmontese massacre is mere English. Milton writes 'scatter'd', 'kept', 'stocks and stones' where another writer might have written 'dispersed', 'preserved', 'effigies'. What is Latin is that 'Forget not', wrenched back to the very end of the first sentence. This anticipates the great opening sentence of *Paradise Lost* which gives a similar sense of titanic effort partly by placing the verb in its Latin rather than its English position. Milton has learned from the Italians the principle of *latinità in volgare*, that is, the disposition of rugged, native vocabulary in an

[1] None of what follows applies to the first Sonnet, 'O nightingale'.

alien idiom, as the Florentine nobles built their Renaissance *palazzi* of undressed stones. All his life Milton had been interested in technical methods of producing tension. In his early *On the Death of a Fair Infant* he imitated what may be called (by a metrical term borrowed from Virgilian scholarship) the Spenserian heterodyne. The heterodyne of a Virgilian hexameter is the tension or sense of collision which can be produced in it by imposing Greek metre on a language for which it was not designed. In Spenser a similar effect is achieved by deliberately stressing a syllable normally unaccented, e.g.

> Those lámping éyes will déigne sometímes to lóok
> (*Amoretti*, 1)

I have marked the metrical stresses. One of them falls on the second syllable of 'sometimes'. But in ordinary speech the accent falls on the first syllable of this word. The resulting heterodyne could easily have been removed, by writing:

> Those lámping éyes will sómetimes déigne to lóok.

But, so altered, the line has lost all its distinctive Spenserian music. In *On the Death of a Fair Infant* Milton caught this music in the line:

> Soft silken primrose fading timelessly

where the normally unstressed last syllable of 'timelessly' has been made to carry a metrical stress. One could remove the heterodyne by writing:

> Soft silken primrose fading ere her time.

In the Sonnets Milton devised, so to speak, a new sort of heterodyne, consisting in the conflict of vocabulary and idiom. The result is, of course, a limbo-language, which was never, and never could be, a part of ordinary speech. Johnson was right when he saw[1] that the remark which Jonson made of Spenser, that he 'wrote no language' was more truly applicable to Milton's 'Babylonish dialect'. There will always be some readers who will detest what Milton did. The keen delight of such unnatural opposition of language will never be widely felt.

Milton has also learned from the Italians the notion of *asprezza*, that is of imparting a roughness to his verse by writing sentences which refuse to co-operate with the line-lengths. His full-stops tend just to miss the line-endings. Thus 'Forget not' in the Piedmont Sonnet is not only a Latinism. It is also a studied insult to the metrical rhythm—in short, yet another sort of heterodyne, the conflict being between the metrical and the sense-unit.

I am conscious that such unity as is to be found in this introduction has been achieved at some cost to a proper comprehensiveness. In stressing formal and stylistic elements I have neglected ideas, images, insights. My excuse must be that I have chosen to explain what seemed to me most difficult, rather than what was intrinsically most import-ant. Many of the most ravishingly beautiful passages of Milton's verse require no critical commentary. One should remember that, even if Milton saw nature 'through the spectacles of books', spectacles are commonly an aid to vision. If Milton distorts reality it is often to magnify or intensify. It is no accident that looking through a teles-scope (quite literally) was for Milton the poet a formative experience. The measureless vacuity of space traversed by Satan in *Paradise Lost* springs from an experience of the poet, even if from an experience artificially intensified. Of Donne's and Milton's reactions to the new astronomy of Copernicus and Galileo, it is Milton's which is the more sensuous.[2] Milton was also capable of a sharp observation at a more prosaic level—for example the passage on the sheep all turning their

[1] In his 'Life of Milton', *Lives of the English Poets* (1783) ed. G. B. Hill, Oxford, 1905, I, pp. 190-1

[2] See Marjorie Nicolson *Science and Imagination* New York, 1956.

faces towards the man as he walks through the field in the Latin *Epitaph for Damon* (66–7). But in general, the inner world is more to Milton than the outer. The personal preoccupations of this formidably learned poet sometimes find their way into the verse in an almost childishly direct fashion. Dalila's lines (*Samson Agonistes*, 903–4)

> In argument with men a woman ever
> Goes by the worse, whatever be her cause.

have every appearance of being a dislocated fragment of real life, retained by an irritated husband.

But, in general, I have treated the poems less as windows opening on a reality separable from themselves than as autonomous constructions. I should like to think that this is the approach Milton himself would have liked best. It follows that those critics who reprove Milton for cultivating language at the expense of reality will scarcely consider themselves answered, for, on their own terms, they have not been. Instead, they are here invited to try a different criterion. The word 'poet' originally meant, not 'describer' but 'maker'. The poems of Milton, though partially opaque, are themselves fully human objects, and as such worthy of attention and love. If we do not always feel, through the poems, the pressure of reality, we always feel the pressure of the poems themselves. Every line by Milton is, in fact, a solid addition to the sum of reality. He did not analyse humanity; he extended it.

The Minor Poems
in English

The Fifth Ode of Horace Book I

There is no real clue to the date of this experiment. Its being first printed in the 1673 edition does not necessarily mean composition after 1645, since two poems of 1628 were first printed in 1673. Nor does its being placed after the sonnets provide any firm ground for conjecture. It is hard to imagine Milton in the 1640s or later being diverted by Pyrrha from more urgent and exalted concerns. Possibly the piece was an offshoot of Milton's practice with Horatian meters in his elegies on the bishop of Ely and the Vice-Chancellor of Cambridge (although the autumn of 1626 is overloaded with longer poems, and in style the ode is unlike the youthful Milton). The translation has received some high praise, but it may be thought that Milton only partly overcame the combined difficulties of extreme literalness and the original metre (fourth Asclepiadean). Some good phrases stand out from the prevailing stiffness—which in lines 9–11 becomes ambiguous awkwardness.

Note: In the notes on the verse the following abbreviations are used:

P.L.   *Paradise Lost*
P.R.   *Paradise Regained*
F.Q.   *Faerie Queene*

Ad Pyrrham   Ode V

Horatius ex Pyrrhae illecebris tanquam e naufragio enataverat, cuius amore irretitos, affirmat esse miseros.

> Quis multa gracilis te puer in rosa
> Perfusus liquidis urget odoribus,
>   Grato, Pyrrha, sub antro?
>   Cui flavam religas comam
> Simplex munditie? heu quoties fidem   5
> Mutatosque deos flebit, et aspera
>   Nigris aequora ventis
>   Emirabitur insolens,
> Qui nunc te fruitur credulus aurea:
> Qui semper vacuam, semper amabilem   10
>   Sperat, nescius aurae
>   Fallacis. miseri quibus
> Intentata nites. me tabula sacer
> Votiva paries indicat uvida
>   Suspendisse potenti   15
>   Vestimenta maris Deo.

The Horatian text, as Milton printed it along with his English, has several variants from modern orthodoxy: the singular *munditie* instead of the plural and *quoties* instead of *quotiens* (line 5), and *Intentata* instead of *Intemptata* (13). Milton's text of the poem and also the Latin headnote are verbally identical with those in the editions of Horace edited by John Bond in 1620 and 1630; the differences in Milton—*v* in place of *u* and commas around Pyrrha—are trifles within the compositor's scope. While two of the cited variants appear in other men's editions of these and earlier years (so far as I have explored), Bond alone seems to have *munditie* (and his 1614 edition has *munditiis*). Apparently, then, the text Milton used was available from at least 1620 onward (I have not seen Bond's earliest editions, but in this case they do not matter).

Quis multa gracilis te puer in rosa render'd almost word for word without rime according to the Latin measure, as near as the language will permit.

What slender youth bedew'd with liquid odours
Courts thee on roses in some pleasant cave,
   Pyrrha? for whom bind'st thou
   In wreaths thy golden hair,
Plain in thy neatness? O how oft shall he   5
On faith and changed gods complain: and seas
   Rough with black winds and storms
   Unwonted shall admire:
Who now enjoys thee credulous, all gold,
Who always vacant, always amiable   10
   Hopes thee; of flattering gales
   Unmindful. Hapless they
To whom thou untri'd seem'st fair. Me in my vow'd
Picture the sacred wall declares t' have hung
   My dank and dropping weeds   15
   To the stern god of sea.

                        (c. 1626–8?)

On the Death of a Fair Infant Dying of a Cough

Anno aetatis 17 [19]

Apart from the Psalms (and Horatian ode?), this is Milton's earliest extant poem in English; it was first printed in the second edition of the *Poems* (1673). The year of his age was apparently a printer's mistake or his own. The infant was his sister Anne Phillips', and the first known death in her family was that of the daughter who was born in January, 1626, and died in January, 1628, when Milton was nineteen. The writing of such a piece was natural enough for a young poet who had done four Latin poems on the death of conspicuous elders, and in this case he could not feel much more personal loss (however much he sympathised with the parents); there was the further difficulty that little could be said about an infant's soul and experience. But in filling the void with mythology and rhetoric, as in the Latin poems, Milton carried classical reference to more functional complexity, developing the contrast between the inadequacy of the pagan vision of death and the full assurance of Christian consolation.

The stanza, which was to appear again in the prelude of the *Nativity* and in *The Passion*, was used by the Spenserian Phineas Fletcher in poems not published until 1633 (Milton might possibly have seen them in manuscript, but he was not less capable than Fletcher of invention); it may be described as a Spenserian stanza with the fifth and sixth lines omitted, or as rhyme royal with a final Alexandrine. Milton's compound adjectives perhaps point to Sylvester. But the fluidity and decorative sweetness of the texture belong to the larger Elizabethan tradition, especially the Spenserian.

1–2 While the idea is traditional, critics cite *The Passionate Pilgrim* (1599), sonnet 10: 'Sweet rose, fair flower, untimely plucked, soon vaded,/Plucked in the bud, and vaded in the spring.' **timelessly** unseasonably

5–7 A common conceit, e.g., Sidney, *Astrophel and Stella* 22.14; Shakespeare, *Venus and Adonis* 1110

8 Aquilo, the north wind (the Greek Boreas), carried off the Athenian princess Orithyia

22–8 Cf. Spenser, *F.Q.* 3.6.45.

I

O fairest flower no sooner blown but blasted,
Soft silken primrose fading timelessly,
Summer's chief honour if thou hadst outlasted
Bleak winter's force that made thy blossom dry;
For he being amorous on that lovely dye   5
   That did thy cheek envermeil, thought to kiss
But kill'd alas, and then bewail'd his fatal bliss.

II

For since grim Aquilo his charioteer
By boist'rous rape th' Athenian damsel got,
He thought it touch'd his deity full near,   10
If likewise he some fair one wedded not,
Thereby to wipe away th' infamous blot
   Of long-uncoupled bed, and childless eld,
Which 'mongst the wanton gods a foul reproach was held.

III

So mounting up in icy-pearled car,   15
Through middle empire of the freezing air
He wander'd long, till thee he spi'd from far,
There ended was his quest, there ceas'd his care.
Down he descended from his snow-soft chair,
   But all unwares with his cold-kind embrace   20
Unhous'd thy virgin soul from her fair biding-place.

IV

Yet art thou not inglorious in thy fate;
For so Apollo, with unweeting hand
Whilom did slay his dearly-loved mate

25   Eurotas a river in Laconia

39   first-moving sphere the *primum mobile*, the tenth and outermost sphere (within the hard outer shell of the universe) which kept the inner spheres in motion

47   Earth's sons the Giants who tried to overthrow the gods

Young Hyacinth born on Eurotas' strand,   25
Young Hyacinth the pride of Spartan land;
  But then transform'd him to a purple flower;
Alack that so to change thee winter had no power.

V

Yet can I not persuade me thou art dead
Or that thy corse corrupts in earth's dark womb,   30
Or that thy beauties lie in wormy bed,
Hid from the world in a low-delved tomb;
Could heav'n for pity thee so strictly doom?
  Oh no! for something in thy face did shine
Above mortality that show'd thou wast divine.   35

VI

Resolve me then O soul most surely blest
(If so it be that thou these plaints dost hear)
Tell me bright spirit where'er thou hoverest
Whether above that high first-moving sphere
Or in th' Elysian fields (if such there were).   40
  O say me true if thou wert mortal wight
And why from us so quickly thou didst take thy flight.

VII

Wert thou some star which from the ruin'd roof
Of shak'd Olympus by mischance didst fall;
Which careful Jove in nature's true behoof   45
Took up, and in fit place did reinstall?
Or did of late Earth's sons besiege the wall
  Of sheeny heav'n, and thou some goddess fled
Amongst us here below to hide thy nectar'd head?

50   maid Astraea, goddess of justice who left the earth after man grew corrupt and became Virgo in the zodiac

53   To fill out a defective line (presumably due to a printer's error), editors have commonly supplied 'Mercy' (cf. *Nativity* 141–6); 'youth' seems to be female. 'Virtue' and 'Peace' have also been suggested (cf. Milton's Prolusion 4 for the linking of Astraea, Peace, and Truth), but 'Peace' by itself would be unmetrical.

57   host angels

66   his God's

VIII

Or wert thou that just maid who once before 50
Forsook the hated earth, O tell me sooth
And cam'st again to visit us once more?
Or wert thou mercy that sweet smiling youth?
Or that crown'd matron sage white-robed truth?
   Or any other of that heav'nly brood 55
Let down in clowdy throne to do the world some good?

IX

Or wert thou of the golden-winged host,
Who having clad thyself in human weed
To earth from thy prefixed seat didst post,
And after short abode fly back with speed, 60
As if to show what creatures heav'n doth breed,
   Thereby to set the hearts of men on fire
To scorn the sordid world, and unto heav'n aspire?

X

But O why didst thou not stay here below
To bless us with thy heav'n-lov'd innocence, 65
To slake his wrath whom sin hath made our foe
To turn swift-rushing black perdition hence,
Or drive away the slaughtering pestilence,
   To stand 'twixt us and our deserved smart?
But thou canst best perform that office where thou art. 70

XI

Then thou the mother of so sweet a child
Her false imagin'd loss cease to lament,
And wisely learn to curb thy sorrows wild;

76-7 Anne Phillips was about to give birth to another child (Elizabeth, baptised April 9, 1628); but Milton seems rather to be thinking of the immortality, promised to the faithful, which is better than children (Isa. 56.5).

Think what a present thou to God hast sent,
And render him with patience what he lent; 75
   This if thou do he will an offspring give,
That till the worlds last end shall make thy name to live.

(1628)

At a Vacation Exercise in the College, Part Latin, Part English

In July, 1628, Milton acted as 'Father' or 'Dictator' at a College assembly which, coming just before the long vacation, was both academic and festive. His Latin speech, printed as his sixth Prolusion, carried on this double vein. The nature of the occasion and his office for the day—an evidence of his growing popularity—prompted a genially urbane discourse; the latter half of it was a less happy effort in the kind of humour expected at such a time. Then followed these English verses, in which Milton took his hearers into his confidence. His poetry hitherto had been almost wholly in Latin. Now he salutes his native language, avows his distaste for the trifling themes and eccentric style of some student poets, and goes on, in couplets of more smoothness and eloquence, to sketch the 'graver' subjects that attract him—nature and the cosmos and 'kings and queens and heroes old.' Lines 33–5 invite comparison with parts of Milton's third Prolusion; and in 33–9 he might be said to make over the end of the first book of the *Iliad* in the spirit of Plato's *Phaedrus* 246–7. The lines were first published in the second edition of Milton's *Poems* (1673).

The Latin speeches ended, the English thus began.

Hail native language, that by sinews weak
Didst move my first endeavouring tongue to speak,
And mad'st imperfect words with childish trips,
Half unpronounc'd, slide through my infant lips,
Driving dumb silence from the portal door,   5
Where he had mutely sat two years before:

8 latter later

27 suspect suspicion

33 deep high (cf. *altus*)

37 unshorn the stock classical epithet

Here I salute thee and thy pardon ask
That now I use thee in my latter task:
Small loss it is that thence can come unto thee,
I know my tongue but little grace can do thee: 10
Thou need'st not be ambitious to be first,
Believe me I have thither pack'd the worst:
And, if it happen as I did forecast,
The daintiest dishes shall be serv'd up last.
I pray thee then deny me not thy aid   15
For this same small neglect that I have made:
But haste thee straight to do me once a pleasure,
And from thy wardrobe bring thy chiefest treasure;
Not those new-fangled toys, and trimming slight
Which takes our late fantastics with delight,   20
But cull those richest robes, and gay'st attire
Which deepest spirits, and choicest wits desire:
I have some naked thoughts that rove about
And loudly knock to have their passage out;
And weary of their place do only stay   25
Till thou hast deck'd them in thy best array;
That so they may without suspect or fears
Fly swiftly to this fair assembly's ears;
Yet I had rather, if I were to choose,
Thy service in some graver subject use,   30
Such as may make thee search thy coffers round,
Before thou clothe my fancy in fit sound:
Such where the deep transported mind may soar
Above the wheeling poles, and at heav'n's door
Look in, and see each blissful deity   35
How he before the thunderous throne doth lie,
Listening to what unshorn Apollo sings

40 In old cosmic theory a sphere of fire (the fourth element) was between the sphere of air and the sphere of the moon; thus it could be called a 'watchful' guardian of the changeless supralunary region against the flux of the sublunary world.

42 **lofts** middle air; in tradition the middle layer of the threefold atmosphere surrounding the earth, a region cold, misty, stormy, and the special haunt of demons.

48–52 *Odyssey* 8.73 f., 266 f., 499 f.

53 Cf. Horace, *Od.* 3.3.70

56 **Predicament** one of the ten Aristotelian categories. The primary one is substance, which is subject to and known through the other nine, quantity, quality, relation, etc. Milton, as 'Father,' is Ens, absolute being.

To th' touch of golden wires, while Hebe brings
Immortal nectar to her kingly sire:
Then passing through the spheres of watchful fire,   40
And misty regions of wide air next under,
And hills of snow and lofts of piled thunder,
May tell at length how green-ey'd Neptune raves,
In heav'n's defiance mustering all his waves;
Then sing of secret things that came to pass   45
When beldam Nature in her cradle was;
And last of kings and queens and heroes old,
Such as the wise Demodocus once told
In solemn songs at King Alcinous' feast,
While sad Ulysses' soul and all the rest   50
Are held with his melodious harmony
In willing chains and sweet captivity.
But fie my wand'ring Muse how thou dost stray!
Expectance calls thee now another way,
Thou know'st it must be now thy only bent   55
To keep in compass of thy Predicament:
Then quick about thy purpos'd business come,
That to the next I may resign my room.

*Then Ens is represented as Father of the Predicaments his ten Sons,
whereof the eldest stood for Substance with his canons, which Ens
thus speaking, explains.*

Good luck befriend thee Son; for at thy birth
The faëry ladies danc'd upon the hearth;   60
Thy drowsy nurse hath sworn she did them spy
Come tripping to the room where thou didst lie;
And sweetly singing round about thy bed
Strew all their blessings on thy sleeping head.

71   A glass for foreseeing the future

91   Rivers the name of one of the students representing the Predicaments.
92 f.   With the possible exception of the Dun, Milton's rivers are all among those catalogued in Spenser, *Faerie Queene* 4.11.24–47 (and full notes are in the Variorum edition of Spenser); there were also descriptions in prose.
92   Ouse probably the midland river that flows into the Wash; see *F.Q.*, **stanza 34 and 37.6**

She heard them give thee this, that thou shouldst still   65
From eyes of mortals walk invisible;
Yet there is something that doth force my fear,
For once it was my dismal hap to hear
A Sybil old, bow-bent with crooked age,
That far events full wisely could presage,   70
And in time's long and dark prospective glass
Foresaw what future days should bring to pass;
Your son, said she (nor can you it prevent),
Shall subject be to many an accident.
O'er all his brethren he shall reign as king,   75
Yet every one shall make him underling,
And those that cannot live from him asunder
Ungratefully shall strive to keep him under;
In worth and excellence he shall outgo them,
Yet being above them, he shall be below them;   80
From others he shall stand in need of nothing,
Yet on his brothers shall depend for clothing.
To find a foe it shall not be his hap,
And peace shall lull him in her flow'ry lap;
Yet shall he live in strife, and at his door   85
Devouring war shall never cease to roar:
Yea it shall be his natural property
To harbour those that are at enmity.
What power, what force, what mighty spell, if not
Your learned hands, can loose this Gordian knot?   90

*The next, Quantity and Quality, spake in prose, then Relation
was call'd by his Name.*

Rivers arise; whether thou be the son
Of utmost Tweed, or Ouse, or gulfy Dun,

93–4   Trent . . . . thirty arms cf. *F.Q.* 35.9, 'thirty sundry streames'

95   Mole . . . underneath: cf. *F.Q.* 32.8–9
96   Severn cf. *F.Q.* 30.6 and *Comus* 824 f.
97   rocky Avon cf. *F.Q.* 31.6–9
98   Tyne the river that has Newcastle at its mouth and flows through a coal-mining region   **hallowed Dee** the river that empties into the Irish Sea near Chester; see *F.Q.* 39.3–4
99   Humber a legendary Scythian king who, after unsuccessfully invading Britain, was drowned in the Humber; cf. *F.Q.* 30.7, 37.8–9, 38

Or Trent, who like some earth-born giant spreads
His thirty arms along th' indented meads,
Or sullen Mole that runneth underneath, 95
Or Severn swift, guilty of maiden's death,
Or rocky Avon, or of sedgy Lee,
Or coaly Tyne, or ancient hallow'd Dee,
Or Humber loud that keeps the Scythian's name,
Or Medway smooth, or royal-tow'red Thame. 100
The rest was prose.
(1628)

Song On May Morning

This lyric, a miniature choral song, is in substance a distillation of Elegy 5. If the conjectural 1629–30 is correct, the poem may be said to inaugurate the Jonsonian vein more amply displayed in the *Epitaph on the Marchioness of Winchester* and *L'Allegro* and *Il Penseroso*. In contrast with, say, the rich colour and detail of Spenser, or the extravagant conceits and compound epithets of Sylvester, Milton's manner is one of restrained and elegant simplicity and urbanity.

Now the bright morning star, day's harbinger,
Comes dancing from the East, and leads with her
The flow'ry May, who from her green lap throws
The yellow cowslip, and the pale primrose.
   Hail bounteous May that dost inspire   5
   Mirth and youth, and warm desire,
   Woods and groves are of thy dressing,
   Hill and dale doth boast thy blessing.
Thus we salute thee with our early song,
And welcome thee, and wish thee long.   10

               (1629–30?)

On the Morning of Christ's Nativity

Milton's first great English poem, one of the great English odes, was written at Christmas, 1629, a few weeks after his twenty-first birthday. While its youthful exuberance may not be quite flawless, the little adverse criticism it has received—on its slighting of the Gospel story, its supposedly artificial conceits, and its supposedly monotonous rhythm—may be thought mostly wrongheaded. Milton's theme is the idea of the Incarnation, its significance as a religious and historical event. The young poet is already a master of form. The prelude states the central, traditional paradox, the contrast between the human infant and his divine power, and links the poet, writing before dawn in London, with 'the star-led wizards' on their way to Bethlehem. The first eight stanzas of the hymn give the cosmic and historical setting: nature, conscious of her imperfections, awaits the advent of her Creator (the conceits belong to the old religious view of half-animate nature and are quite distinct from 'the pathetic fallacy'). In the second movement the angelic music, blending with the music of the spheres, announces the new and closer harmony between heaven and earth; it also recalls the music of Creation, the first supreme event, and then casts forward to the third event, the Day of Judgement. Since the Incarnation prepares the way for redemption and eternity, the third movement describes the first stage in fallen man's recovery of truth and righteousness, the overthrow of the pagan gods and idolatrous religions—a bravura passage in which the young poet is somewhat carried away by his first grand orchestration of exotic names. Here, and throughout, images of darkness and discord are in contrast with the dominant images of light and music. This poem has the first of Milton's great quiet endings: in two narrative and pictorial lines of subtle simplicity he reasserts the central

6 sages the Old Testament prophets

8–14 Phil. 2.6–8

11 trinal unity the Trinity

paradox and the central theme of order and the new bond between heaven and man.

The style is much more Miltonic than it was in the *Death of a Fair Infant* of less than a year before, but it is still in the Spenserian tradition. The tone ranges from the sweet to the plangent. The stanzaic form used in the prelude is that of the *Fair Infant*; the stanza of the hymn may be Milton's own invention. While the internal music of the stanzas varies a good deal, the comparative regularity of the pattern may seem wholly appropriate to a song of jubilation. Along with the Bible many things may have made general or particular contributions, from Virgil's fourth or 'Messianic' eclogue to Tasso's *Canzone Sopra la Cappella del Presepio* and Giles Fletcher's *Christ's Victory and Triumph* (1610). In his *Poems* of 1645 Milton placed the *Nativity* first. (On the ode, see also below, p. 343 ff.).

I

This is the month, and this the happy morn
Wherein the Son of heav'n's eternal King,
Of wedded maid, and virgin mother born,
Our great redemption from above did bring;
For so the holy sages once did sing,   5
    That he our deadly forfeit should release,
And with his Father work us a perpetual peace.

II

That glorious form, that light unsufferable,
And that far-beaming blaze of majesty,
Wherewith he wont at heav'n's high council-table,   10
To sit the midst of trinal unity,
He laid aside; and here with us to be,
    Forsook the courts of everlasting day,
And chose with us a darksome house of mortal clay.

21   The stars above London become the angelic host above the shepherds. Throughout the hymn the mixture of tenses telescopes past and present.

23   wizards the Magi or three wise men (Matt. 2.1 f.)

28   Isa. 6.6–7

35–6   Cf. Elegy 5.55f.

III

Say heav'nly Muse, shall not thy sacred vein   15
Afford a present to the infant God?
Hast thou no verse, no hymn, or solemn strain,
To welcome him to this his new abode,
Now while the heav'n by the sun's team untrod,
   Hath took no print of the approaching light,   20
And all the spangled host keep watch in squadrons bright?

IV

See how from far upon the eastern road
The star-led wizards haste with odours sweet:
O run, prevent them with thy humble ode,
And lay it lowly at his blessed feet;   25
Have thou the honour first, thy Lord to greet,
   And join thy voice unto the angel choir,
From out his secret altar touch'd with hallow'd fire.

THE HYMN

I

It was the winter wild,
While the heav'n-born-child,   30
   All meanly wrapp'd in the rude manger lies;
Nature in awe to him
Had doff'd her gaudy trim,
   With her great master so to sympathise:
It was no season then for her   35
To wanton with the sun, her lusty paramour.

42 Rev. 3.18

46–52 Peace is described as if a figure in a contemporary masque. Cf. 141–8.
47 olive a symbol of peace
48 sphere the firmament, which in the old astronomy turned daily about
the earth

50 turtle turtle dove

52–60 Christian writers (e.g., Augustine, *City of God* 18.46) saw a fulfilment
of Old Testament prophecy in the peace prevailing in the Roman empire at
the time of Christ's birth.

56 hooked with projecting blades

II

Only with speeches fair
She woos the gentle Air
  To hide her guilty front with innocent snow,
And on her naked shame,   40
Pollute with sinful blame,
  The saintly veil of maiden white to throw,
Confounded, that her maker's eyes
Should look so near upon her foul deformities.

III

But he her fears to cease,   45
Sent down the meek-ey'd Peace;
  She crown'd with olive green, came softly sliding
Down through the turning sphere
His ready harbinger,
  With turtle wing the amorous clouds dividing,   50
And waving wide her myrtle wand,
She strikes a universal peace through sea and land.

IV

No war, or battle's sound
Was heard the world around:
  The idle spear and shield were high up hung;   55
The hooked chariot stood
Unstain'd with hostile blood,
  The trumpet spake not to the armed throng,
And kings sat still with awful eye,
As if they surely knew their sov'reign Lord was by.   60

64   whist hushed (cf. the same rhyme in *The Tempest* 1.2.377–8)

68   birds halcyons, whose nesting time at the winter solstice (December 22) was associated with fair weather at sea

74 Lucifer the morning star, Venus. (In Elegy 3.50 and Elegy 5.46 Lucifer is the sun.)

84   Cf. the myth of Phaethon

V

But peaceful was the night
Wherein the Prince of Light
  His reign of peace upon the earth began:
The winds with wonder whist,
Smoothly the waters kiss'd,   65
    Whispering new joys to the mild ocean,
Who now hath quite forgot to rave,
While birds of calm sit brooding on the charmed wave.

VI

The stars with deep amaze
Stand fix'd in steadfast gaze,   70
  Bending one way their precious influence,
And will not take their flight,
For all the morning light,
    Or Lucifer that often warn'd them thence;
But in their glimmering orbs did glow,   75
Until their Lord himself bespake, and bid them go.

VII

And though the shady gloom
Had given day her room,
  The sun himself withheld his wonted speed,
And hid his head for shame,   80
As his inferior flame,
    The new-enlight'n'd world no more should need;
He saw a greater sun appear
Than his bright throne, or burning axle-tree could bear.

86   Or ere before

89   Pan god of shepherds and of nature; in Renaissance poetry sometimes used (as here) for Christ, the good shepherd

90   kindly beneficently and as one of the human race or 'kind'

92   silly simple, innocent

102   round sphere of the moon (Cynthia, Diana)

106   its a word used only three times in Milton's verse: cf. *Paradise Lost* 1.254 and 4.813; elsewhere he uses 'his' or 'her'

VIII

The shepherds on the lawn,   85
Or ere the point of dawn,
   Sat simply chatting in a rustic row;
Full little thought they then,
That the mighty Pan
   Was kindly come to live with them below;   90
Perhaps their loves, or else their sheep,
Was all that did their silly thoughts so busy keep.

IX

When such music sweet
Their hearts and ears did greet,
   As never was by mortal singer strook,   95
Divinely-warbled voice
Answering the stringed noise,
   As all their souls in blisful rapture took:
The air such pleasure loth to lose,
With thousand echoes still prolongs each heav'nly close.   100

X

Nature that heard such sound
Beneath the hollow round
   Of Cynthia's seat, the airy region thrilling,
Now was almost won
To think her part was done,   105
   And that her reign had here its last fulfilling;
She knew such harmony alone
Could hold all heav'n and earth in happier union.

112–13 In medieval tradition there were nine orders: Seraphim, Cherubim, Thrones; Dominations, Virtues, Powers; Principalities, Archangels, Angels. Milton does not use the titles strictly; about two thirds of his angelic names are in the Bible and Apocrypha.

119 Cf. Job 38.6–7 (and *P.L.* 7.252–60)

122 Cf. Job 26.7, Ovid, *Met.* 1.12–13 (and *P.L.* 7.242)

124 Cf. Ovid, *Met.* 1.30–31, 36 f.

125 f. In the Pythagorean-Platonic-Christian tradition the moving spheres of the planets made music which would be audible to the sinless or disembodied soul; cf. Plato, *Rep.* 617; Cicero, *Rep.* 6.17–18; *The Merchant of Venice* 5.1.60–65; Milton, Prolusion 2 and *Arcades* 68 f.

131–2 The music of the nine spheres blending with that of the nine orders of angels

XI

At last surrounds their sight
A globe of circular light, 110
  That with long beams the shame-fac'd night array'd,
The helmed cherubim
And sworded seraphim
  Are seen in glittering ranks with wings display'd,
Harping in loud and solemn choir, 115
With unexpressive notes to heav'n's new-born heir.

XII

Such music (as 'tis said)
Before was never made,
  But when of old the sons of morning sung,
While the creator great 120
His constellations set,
  And the well-ballanc'd world on hinges hung,
And cast the dark foundations deep,
And bid the welt'ring waves their oozy channel keep.

XIII

Ring out ye crystal spheres, 125
Once bless our human ears,
  (If ye have power to touch our senses so)
And let your silver chime
Move in melodious time;
  And let the base of heav'n's deep organ blow, 130
And with your ninefold harmony
Make up full consort to th' angelic symphony.

135 Cf. Virgil, *Ecl.* 4; Ovid, *Met.* 1.89 f.

136 The stains of sin; cf. Horace, *Od.* 4.5.22

140 peering appearing

141–6 A combination of the classical Astraea or Justice (Virgil, *Ecl.* 4.6, Ovid, *Met.* 1.149–50) with Ps. 85.10–11: 'Mercy and Truth are met together; righteousness and peace have kissed each other'

143–4 The 1645 reading (altered in 1673) was: 'Th' enameled arras of the rainbow wearing,/And Mercy set between'.

146 tissued woven, especially with gold or silver thread

151 infancy The word seems to include its literal sense, 'not speaking'.

155–64 The last judgement (cf. *P.L.* 3.323 f.)

155 ychain'd The 'y' is a literary relic of the Old English participial prefix 'ge', a frequent archaism in Spenser. **sleep** death

156 1 Thess. 4.16

XIV

For if such holy song
Enwrap our fancy long,
   Time will run back, and fetch the age of gold,   135
And speckl'd vanity
Will sicken soon and die,
   And leprous sin will melt from earthly mould,
And hell itself will pass away,
And leave her dolorous mansions to the peering day.   140

XV

Yea truth, and justice then
Will down return to men,
   Orb'd in a rainbow; and like glories wearing
Mercy will sit between,
Thron'd in celestial sheen,   145
   With radiant feet the tissued clouds down steering,
And heav'n as at some festival,
Will open wide the gates of her high palace hall.

XVI

But wisest fate says no,
This must not yet be so,   150
   The babe lies yet in smiling infancy,
That on the bitter cross
Must redeem our loss;
   So both himself and us to glorify:
Yet first to those ychain'd in sleep,   155
The wakeful trump of doom must thunder through the deep,

157–9   When Moses received the Ten Commandments (Exod. 19.16–18)

160   Cf. Milton's early *Psalm* 114, line 15
161   Cf. Spenser, *F.Q.* 1.8.4.6, 'the terror of that blast'

164   1 Thess. 4.17

168   dragon Satan (Rev. 12.9, 20.2)

172   Swinges lashes about

173 f.   In Christian tradition the pagan gods were regarded as devils (cf. *P.L.* 1.364 f.); for oracles, cf. *P.R.* 1. 430–64.

XVII

With such a horrid clang
As on Mount Sinai rang
 While the red fire, and smould'ring clouds out brake:
The aged earth aghast   160
With terror of that blast,
 Shall from the surface to the centre shake,
When at the world's last session,
The dreadful judge in middle air shall spread his throne.

XVIII

And then at last our bliss   165
Full and perfect is,
 But now begins; for from this happy day
Th' old dragon under ground
In straiter limits bound,
 Not half so far casts his usurped sway, 170
And wroth to see his kingdom fail,
Swinges the scaly horror of his folded tail.

XIX

The oracles are dumb,
No voice or hideous hum
 Runs through the arched roof in words deceiving. 175
Apollo from his shrine
Can no more divine,
 With hollow shriek the steep of Delphos leaving.
No nightly trance, or breathed spell,
Inspires the pale-ey'd priest from the prophetic cell. 180

191   **lars** *Lares*, Roman tutelary gods of the home   **lemures** spirits of the dead

194   **flamens** ancient Roman priests
195   **sweat** cf. Virgil, *Georg.* 1.480

197–213   Heathen deities

199   Dagon, a Philistine god

XX

The lonely mountains o'er,
And the resounding shore,
 A voice of weeping heard, and loud lament;
From haunted spring, and dale
Edg'd with poplar pale,   185
 The parting genius is with sighing sent;
With flow'r-inwov'n tresses torn
The nymphs in twilight shade of tangled thickets mourn.

XXI

In consecrated earth,
And on the holy hearth,   190
 The lars, and lemures moan with midnight plaint;
In urns, and altars round,
A drear, and dying sound
 Affrights the flamens at their service quaint;
And the chill marble seems to sweat,   195
While each peculiar power forgoes his wonted seat.

XXII

Peor, and Baalim,
Forsake their temples dim,
 With that twice batter'd god of Palestine,
And mooned Ashtaroth,   200
Heav'n's queen and mother both,
 Now sits not girt with tapers' holy shine,
The Libyc Hammon shrinks his horn,
In vain the Tyrian maids their wounded Thammuz mourn.

212   Anubis an Egyptian god, son of Osiris, represented with a jackal's head

215   unshow'r'd without rain

219   timbrell'd accompanied by tambourines
220   sable-stoled black-robed

223   eyn (archaic) eyes

227–8 In spite of the anti-pagan context, the lines suggest the infant Hercules strangling the serpents.

XXIII

And sullen Moloch fled,   205
Hath left in shadows dread
  His burning idol all of blackest hue;
In vain with cymbals' ring,
They call the grisly king,
  In dismal dance about the furnace blue;   210
The brutish gods of Nile as fast,
Isis and Orus, and the dog Anubis haste.

XXIV

Nor is Osiris seen
In Memphian grove, or green,
  Trampling th' unshower'd grass with lowings loud: 215
Nor can he be at rest
Within his sacred chest,
  Nought but profoundest hell can be his shroud;
In vain with timbrell'd anthems dark
The sable-stoled sorcerers bear his worshipp'd ark.   220

XXV

He feels from Juda's land
The dreaded infant's hand,
  The rays of Bethlehem blind his dusky eyn;
Nor all the gods beside,
Longer dare abide,   225
  Not Typhon huge ending in snaky twine:
Our babe to show his Godhead true,
Can in his swaddling bands control the damned crew.

232–6   Cf. *A Midsummer Night's Dream* 3.2.378–87; *Hamlet* 1.1.149–55

236   Night had a chariot corresponding to that of Dawn.

240   **youngest teemed**   latest born
241   Matt. 2.9

243–4   Cf. 30–31

XXVI

So when the sun in bed,
Curtain'd with cloudy red, 230
   Pillows his chin upon an orient wave,
The flocking shadows pale
Troop to th' infernal jail,
   Each fetter'd ghost slips to his several grave,
And the yellow-skirted fays 235
Fly after the night-steeds, leaving their moon-lov'd maze.

XXVII

But see the virgin blest,
Hath laid her babe to rest.
   Time is our tedious song should here have ending:
Heav'n's youngest teemed star 240
Hath fix'd her polish'd car,
   Her sleeping Lord with handmaid lamp attending,
And all about the courtly stable,
Bright-harness'd angels sit in order serviceable.

(1629)

13–14 Cf. Hercules

15–16 Heb. 1.9, 9.11

The Passion

Since the first stanza of this poem alludes to the *Nativity*, it was presumably written just before the following Easter, 1630. The inspiration of the *Nativity* probably led to an uninspired resolution to follow it up. *The Passion* has some beautiful lines but, instead of getting into its subject, it wanders further and further away. Milton's note at the end, the only note of its kind, indicates his dissatisfaction.

I

Erewhile of music, and ethereal mirth,
Wherewith the stage of air and earth did ring,
And joyous news of heav'nly infant's birth,
My muse with angels did divide to sing;
But headlong joy is ever on the wing,   5
   In wintry solstice like the short'n'd light
Soon swallow'd up in dark and long out-living night.

II

For now to sorrow must I tune my song,
And set my harp to notes of saddest woe,
Which on our dearest Lord did seize ere long   10
Dangers, and snares, and wrongs, and worse than so,
Which he for us did freely undergo:
   Most perfect hero, tri'd in heaviest plight
Of labours huge and hard, too hard for human wight.

III

He sov'reign priest stooping his regal head   15
That dropp'd with odorous oil down his fair eyes,

26   The *Christiad*, a Latin epic on the life of Christ by M. G. Vida (1485–1566) of Cremona

28   **still** subdued

37   **prophet** Ezekiel 1

39   **Salem** Jerusalem

Poor fleshly tabernacle entered,
His starry front low-roof'd beneath the skies;
O what a mask was there, what a disguise!
   Yet more; the stroke of death he must abide,   20
Then lies him meekly down fast by his brethren's side.

IV

These latter scenes confine my roving verse,
To this horizon is my Phoebus bound;
His godlike acts, and his temptations fierce,
And former sufferings otherwhere are found;   25
Loud o'er the rest Cremona's trump doth sound;
   Me softer airs befit, and softer strings
Of lute, or viol still, more apt for mournful things.

V

Befriend me night, best patroness of grief,
Over the pole thy thickest mantle throw,   30
And work my flatter'd fancy to belief,
That heav'n and earth are colour'd with my woe;
My sorrows are too dark for day to know:
   The leaves should all be black whereon I write,
And letters where my tears have wash'd a wannish white.   35

VI

See, see the chariot, and those rushing wheels
That whirl'd the prophet up at Chebar flood;
My spirit some transporting cherub feels,
To bear me where the towers of Salem stood,
Once glorious towers, now sunk in guiltless blood;   40
   There doth my soul in holy vision sit

43   rock Christ's tomb (Matt. 27.60 and the other Gospels)

46   quarry stone

51 Jer. 9.10

56 Cf. Ixion a Greek king who, taken to heaven by Zeus, attempted to make love to Hera, but, through Zeus's contrivance, embraced a phantom and begot a centaur.

In pensive trance, and anguish, and ecstatic fit.

VII
Mine eye hath found that sad sepulchral rock
That was the casket of heav'n's richest store,
And here though grief my feeble hands up lock,   45
Yet on the soft'n'd quarry would I score
My plaining verse as lively as before;
    For sure so well instructed are my tears,
That they would fitly fall in order'd characters.

VIII
Or should I thence hurried on viewless wing,   50
Take up a weeping on the mountains wild,
The gentle neighbourhood of grove and spring
Would soon unbosom all their echoes mild,
And I (for grief is easily beguil'd)
    Might think th' infection of my sorrows loud   55
Had got a race of mourners on some pregnant cloud.

This subject the author finding to be above the years he had,
when he wrote it, and nothing satisfi'd with what was begun,
left it unfinished.

                                                        (1630)

1–2   Cf. Elegy 5.25–26

4   jolly hours cf. *Iliad*. 21.450

Sonnet I

Milton's first English sonnet, written in the spring of perhaps 1630, is somewhat akin to Elegy VII (though far from expressing any intense feeling) and much more to the Italian sonnets that follow. It may indeed have been an experimental prelude to amatory ventures in another language. The sonnet is a piece of graceful artifice, half humorous in its use of the medieval fancy that, if a lover in springtime heard the nightingale before the cuckoo, he would be successful in love.

O nightingale, that on yon bloomy spray
   Warbl'st at eve, when all the woods are still,
   Thou with fresh hope the lover's heart dost fill,
   While the jolly hours lead on propitious May;
Thy liquid notes that close the eye of day,   5
   First heard before the shallow cuckoo's bill
   Portend success in love; O if Jove's will
   Have link'd that amorous power to thy soft lay,
Now timely sing, ere the rude bird of hate
   Foretell my hopeless doom in some grove nigh: 10
   As thou from year to year hast sung too late
For my relief; yet hadst no reason why.
   Whether the muse, or love call thee his mate,
   Both them I serve, and of their train am I.
                     (1629–30?)

1 (and **6**)   **What** Why

4   See the note on *Nativity* 155. The archaic 'y' does not belong with a present participle.
5   **son of memory** i.e. brother of the Muses

On Shakespeare

This poem—Milton's first English one to be published—was printed in and presumably written for the Second Folio of Shakespeare (1632); it may have been requested by the printer. Such a tribute, in addition to some specific allusions, is welcome evidence of the young poet's recognition of Shakespeare, and is a partial confirmation of many apparent echoes in Milton's poetry. The conception of Shakespeare as an untutored natural genius (lines 9–10) became current quite early, for example in Jonson's poem in the First Folio (1623), although Jonson praised his art also (cf. *L'Allegro* 131–4). Milton doubtless remembered Jonson's line (22): 'Thou art a monument, without a tomb.' He may have known and consciously echoed an epitaph on Sir Edward Stanley which was ascribed to Shakespeare:

> Not monumental stones preserves our fame;
> Nor sky-aspiring pyramids our name;
> The memory of him for whom this stands
> Shall outlive marble and defacers' hands . . .

The general idea is as old as Horace, *Odes* 3.30.

What needs my Shakespeare for his honour'd bones,
The labour of an age in piled stones,
Or that his hallow'd relics should be hid
Under a star-ypointing pyramid?
Dear son of memory, great heir of fame,   5
What need'st thou such weak witness of thy name?
Thou in our wonder and astonishment
Hast built thyself a live-long monument.

11   unvalu'd invaluable

14   Cf. *Il Penseroso* 42 and William Browne, *On the Countess Dowager of Pembroke:*

> Marble piles let no man raise
> To her name, for after-days
> Some kind woman, born as she,
> Reading this, like Niobe
> Shall turn marble, and become
> Both her mourner and her tomb.

For whilst to th' shame of slow-endeavouring art,
Thy easy numbers flow, and that each heart   10
Hath from the leaves of thy unvalu'd book
Those Delphic lines with deep impression took,
Then thou our fancy of itself bereaving,
Dost make us marble with too much conceiving;
And so sepulchred in such pomp dost lie,   15
That kings for such a tomb would wish to die.

(1630)

1 girt saddle-girth

On the University Carrier

who sick'n'd in the time of his vacancy, being forbid to go to London, by reason of the plague

Thomas Hobson, who kept a livery in Cambridge and whose system of hiring out horses gave birth to the phrase 'Hobson's choice,' for over sixty years drove a wagon weekly between Cambridge and London. He had to stop, at the age of about 86, in the spring of 1630, when Cambridge was quarantined by the plague. He died on January 1, 1631, and many students wrote verses of affectionate jocosity in memory of the well-known veteran. Milton's second poem—more closely packed with puns than the other—was first printed, with variations, in the sixth edition of an anthology, *A Banquet of Jests* (1640), and both were included in *Wit Restor'd* (1658); neither book gave Milton's name. Authentic versions of both pieces were printed in his *Poems* of 1645.

Here lies old Hobson, Death hath broke his girt,
And here alas, hath laid him in the dirt,
Or else the ways being foul, twenty to one,
He's here stuck in a slough, and overthrown.
'Twas such a shifter, that if truth were known,   5
Death was half glad when he had got him down;
For he had any time this ten years full,
Dodg'd with him, betwixt Cambridge and the Bull.
And surely, Death could never have prevail'd,
Had not his weekly course of carriage fail'd;   10

But lately finding him so long at home,
And thinking now his journey's end was come,
And that he had ta'en up his latest inn,
In the kind office of a chamberlain
Show'd him his room where he must lodge that night,   15
Pull'd off his boots, and took away the light:
If any ask for him, it shall be said,
Hobson has supp'd, and 's newly gone to bed.

(1631)

5   sphere-metal the indestructible material of the heavens

7   Time . . . motion a traditional commonplace (Plato, *Timaeus* 37–8)

10   principles powers

26   Like convicted persons being pressed to death and longing for a quick end

Another on the Same

Here lieth one who did most truly prove
That he could never die while he could move,
So hung his destiny never to rot
While he might still jog on, and keep his trot,
Made of sphere-metal, never to decay   5
Until his revolution was at stay.
Time numbers motion, yet (without a crime
'Gainst old truth) motion number'd out his time;
And like an engine mov'd with wheel and weight,
His principles being ceas'd, he ended straight.   10
Rest that gives all men life, gave him his death,
And too much breathing put him out of breath;
Nor were it contradiction to affirm
Too long vacation hast'n'd on his term.
Merely to drive the time away he sick'n'd,   15
Fainted, and di'd, nor would with ale be quick'n'd;
Nay, quoth he, on his swooning bed outstretch'd,
If I may not carry, sure I'll ne'er be fetch'd,
But vow though the cross doctors all stood hearers,
For one carrier put down to make six bearers.   20
Ease was his chief disease, and to judge right,
He di'd for heaviness that his cart went light.
His leisure told him that his time was come,
And lack of load made his life burdensome,
That even to his last breath (there be that say't)   25
As he were press'd to death, he cri'd more weight;
But had his doings lasted as they were,

29–31   The ebb and flow of the tides as caused by the moon

He had been an immortal carrier.
Obedient to the moon he spent his date
In course reciprocal, and had his fate   30
Link'd to the mutual flowing of the seas,
Yet (strange to think) his wane was his increase:
His letters are deliver'd all and gone,
Only remains this superscription.

(1631)

An Epitaph on the Marchioness of Winchester

Jane Paulet, wife of the Catholic Marquis of Winchester, died on April 15, 1631, aged twenty-three, after giving birth to a dead boy; the cause of her death was an infected abscess in her cheek. Although the poem contains some biographical details, there is no evidence for Milton's having been acquainted with her or her family; but, since she was not a public figure like a bishop, he would hardly have written such a poem without any warrant. Possibly some Cambridge poets planned a collection of elegies. Though slighter than Henry King's great *Exequy*, and of course not inspired by any such personal grief, Milton's poem on the premature death of a noble and exemplary young wife and mother has lines of comparable tenderness and poignancy. This was his first poem in couplets of seven or eight syllables and mixed iambics and trochaics—the pattern to be used with even finer felicity in *L'Allegro* and *Il Penseroso*. The poem also inaugurated a new phase in the evolution of Milton's style; its Jonsonian simplicity may be measured by comparison with the Spenserian *Fair Infant* of three years earlier.(Jonson's own elegy on the Marchioness was a somewhat external and declamatory piece.)

This rich marble doth inter
The honour'd wife of Winchester,
A viscount's daughter, an earl's heir,
Besides what her virtues fair
Added to her noble birth,   5
More than she could own from earth.
Summers three times eight save one
She had told, alas too soon,
After so short time of breath,

18   **god** Hymen (cf. *L'Allegro* 125–6)

22   A symbol of death

24   The Marchioness had given birth to a son in 1629, seven years after her marriage.

26   **Lucina** the Roman goddess of childbirth

28   **Atropos** the third of the three Fates, who cut the thread of life

To house with darkness, and with death,   10
Yet had the number of her days
Been as complete as was her praise,
Nature and fate had had no strife
In giving limit to her life.
Her high birth, and her graces sweet   15
Quickly found a lover meet;
The virgin choir for her request
The god that sits at marriage-feast;
He at their invoking came
But with a scarce-well-lighted flame;   20
And in his garland as he stood,
Ye might discern a cypress bud.
Once had the early matrons run
To greet her of a lovely son,
And now with second hope she goes,   25
And calls Lucina to her throes;
But whether by mischance or blame
Atropos for Lucina came;
And with remorseless cruelty,
Spoil'd at once both fruit and tree: 30
The hapless babe before his birth
Had burial, yet not laid in earth,
And the languish'd mother's womb
Was not long a living tomb.
So have I seen some tender slip   35
Sav'd with care from winter's nip,
The pride of her carnation train,
Pluck'd up by some unheedy swain,
Who only thought to crop the flower
New shot up from vernal show'r;   40

47–8 Cf. the dirge in *Cymbeline* (4.2.280–1

50 seize possess

55 perfect sincere

59 Came the river Cam at Cambridge

63 Rachel, Jacob's wife, who died in giving birth to Benjamin (Gen. 29–30 and 35.16–20). Dante had linked Rachel with Beatrice (*Par.* 32.7–9).

But the fair blossom hangs the head
Sideways as on a dying bed,
And those pearls of dew she wears
Prove to be presaging tears
Which the sad morn had let fall   45
On her hast'ning funeral.
Gentle lady may thy grave
Peace and quiet ever have;
After this thy travail sore
Sweet rest seize thee evermore,   50
That to give the world increase,
Short'n'd hast thy own life's lease;
Here besides the sorrowing
That thy noble house doth bring,
Here be tears of perfect moan   55
Wept for thee in Helicon,
And some flowers, and some bays,
For thy hearse to strew the ways,
Sent thee from the banks of Came,
Devoted to thy virtuous name;   60
Whilst thou bright saint high sit'st in glory,
Next her much like to thee in story,
That fair Syrian shepherdess,
Who after years of barrenness
The highly favour'd Joseph bore   65
To him that serv'd for her before,
And at her next birth much like thee,
Through pangs fled to felicity,
Far within the bosom bright
Of blazing majesty and light;   70
There with thee, new welcome saint,

Like fortunes may her soul acquaint,
With thee there clad in radiant sheen,
No marchioness, but now a queen.

(1631)

L'Allegro and Il Penseroso

L'Allegro and *Il Penseroso* may have been written in Milton's last long vacation in 1631, when he was 22, or perhaps in the following summer. They are the most felicitous lyrical products of the young poet's Jonsonian phase, which had begun with the *Epitaph on the Marchioness of Winchester*; along with Jonson's classical symmetry, clarity, and urbanity, the poems have a refined purity of vision, a delicacy and charm of phrase and tone and rhythm, that are beyond the master's reach. The structural line—with contrasting images of light and darkness—is provided by patterns of an ideal day and night, although these short periods overlap and take in different seasons as well as quite diverse scenes. (In his first academic Prolusion, on the comparative superiority of day or night, Milton had remarked that the theme was more suitable for verse than prose.) The two poems, obviously designed as companion pieces, are linked together by constant parallels and contrasts, all governed by 'decorum' and contributing to the unified whole. The universal abstractions, Mirth and Melancholy (the latter is really Contemplation, of an especially Platonic cast), are given substance through outdoor and indoor settings and a variety of allusion, and details are generalised and idealised in keeping with the themes; the picture of meditative and studious solitude is less concrete than the world of people whom the cheerful man observes. Milton's temperament was flexible enough to enable him to distill both states of mind—and Mirth as well as Contemplation has an affinity with heaven. While the twin poems are creations of pure poetry, they remind us of various literary genres, the academic disputation, the pastoral, the 'character', the emblem, and the encomium. Critics have seen an initial suggestion in the verses prefixed to the third edition (1628) of Robert Burton's *Anatomy of Melancholy*; there seem to be echoes of a number of poets, more than the notes can take account of. The metrical pattern of both poems carries on, with appropriate modulations, that of the preceding *Epitaph*.

1–10   The melancholy here banished is not casual depression or the contemplative state celebrated in *Il Penseroso* but the disease recognised in medical tradition.

9   ragged rugged

12   yclept called (see note on *Nativity* 155)   **Euphrosyne** one of the three Graces, who personified the refinements of life

15   Cf. Horace, *Od.* 4.7.5

22   Cf. *Taming of the Shrew* 2.1.174

24   buxom, blithe in *Pericles*, prologue, line 23   **debonair** graceful, gracious

27   cranks odd turns of speech

L'Allegro

Hence loathed Melancholy
   Of Cerberus, and blackest midnight born,
In Stygian cave forlorn
   'Mongst horrid shapes, and shrieks, and sights unholy.
Find out some uncouth cell,   5
   Where brooding darkness spreads his jealous wings,
And the night-raven sings;
   There under ebon shades, and low-brow'd rocks,
As ragged as thy locks,
   In dark Cimmerian desert ever dwell.   10

But come thou goddess fair and free,
In heav'n yclept Euphrosyne,
And by men, heart-easing Mirth,
Whom lovely Venus at a birth
With two sister Graces more   15
To ivy-crowned Bacchus bore;
Or whether (as some sager sing)
The frolic wind that breathes the spring,
Zephyr with Aurora playing,
As he met her once a-Maying,   20
There on beds of violets blue,
And fresh-blown roses wash'd in dew,
Fill'd her with thee a daughter fair,
So buxom, blithe, and debonair.
Haste thee nymph, and bring with thee   25
Jest and youthful Jollity,
Quips and cranks, and wanton wiles,

28 **becks** upward nods

33 **ye** 1673 you

39 Cf. Marlowe's pastoral lyric, 'Come live with me and be my love'

45 The subject of 'to come,' as of the preceding infinitive, is the poet, who greets the new day at his window. **spite** defiance

55 **hoar** grey, from lack of foliage or early morning mist or hoar frost

Nods, and becks, and wreathed smiles,
Such as hang on Hebe's cheek,
And love to live in dimple sleek;   30
Sport that wrinkled Care derides,
And Laughter holding both his sides.
Come, and trip it as ye go
On the light fantastic toe,
And in thy right hand lead with thee   35
The mountain nymph, sweet Liberty;
And if I give thee honour due,
Mirth, admit me of thy crew
To live with her, and live with thee,
In unreproved pleasures free;   40
To hear the lark begin his flight,
And singing startle the dull night,
From his watch-tow'r in the skies,
Till the dappled dawn doth rise;
Then to come in spite of sorrow,   45
And at my window bid good morrow
Through the sweet-briar, or the vine,
Or the twisted eglantine.
While the cock with lively din
Scatters the rear of darkness thin,   50
And to the stack, or the barn door,
Stoutly struts his dames before,
Oft list'ning how the hounds and horn,
Cheerly rouse the slumb'ring morn,
From the side of some hoar hill,   55
Through the high wood echoing shrill.
Sometime walking not unseen
By hedgerow elms, or hillocks green,

59   eastern gate cf. *Midsummer Night's Dream* 3.2.391

60   state stately progress (of Phoebus the sun-god)

67   tells his tale either 'counts his sheep' (as in George Wither, *Fair Virtue* 691), or 'tells his story' (as in Wither, *Shepherd's Hunting*, Ecl. 3.24). In Wither, as in Virgil, *Ecl.* 6.85, the counting is an evening operation; in Virgil, *Ecl.* 3.34 (where Dryden translates 'takes the tale'), it is done twice a day.

70   landscape Milton's word was 'lantskip'

75   pied variegated (cf. *Love's Labour's Lost* 5.2.904)

Right against the eastern gate,
Where the great sun begins his state,   60
Rob'd in flames, and amber light,
The clouds in thousand liveries dight,
While the ploughman near at hand
Whistles o'er the furrow'd land,
And the milkmaid singeth blithe,   65
And the mower whets his scythe,
And every shepherd tells his tale
Under the hawthorn in the dale.
Straight mine eye hath caught new pleasures
Whilst the landscape round it measures   70
Russet lawns, and fallows grey,
Where the nibbling flocks do stray,
Mountains on whose barren breast
The labouring clouds do often rest:
Meadows trim with daisies pied,   75
Shallow brooks, and rivers wide.
Towers, and battlements it sees
Bosom'd high in tufted trees,
Where perhaps some beauty lies,
The cynosure of neighbouring eyes.   80
Hard by, a cottage chimney smokes,
From betwixt two aged oaks,
Where Corydon and Thyrsis met
Are at their savoury dinner set
Of herbs, and other country messes,   85
Which the neat-handed Phillis dresses;
And then in haste her bow'r she leaves,
With Thestylis to bind the sheaves;
Or if the earlier season lead

94   rebecks primitive violins

102 Mab See *Romeo and Juliet* 1.4.53 f.   **eat** past tense

103–4   She, . . . he members of the story-telling group
104   friar's lanthorn will-o'-the-wisp. In 1673 the line read 'And by the
Friar's Lanthorn led'.
105   goblin Robin Goodfellow, Puck.

110   lubber fiend drudging spirit

To the tann'd haycock in the mead,   90
Sometimes with secure delight
The upland hamlets will invite,
When the merry bells ring round,
And the jocund rebecks sound
To many a youth, and many a maid,   95
Dancing in the chequer'd shade;
And young and old come forth to play
On a sunshine holiday,
Till the livelong daylight fail,
Then to the spicy nut-brown ale,   100
With stories told of many a feat,
How Faery Mab the junkets eat;
She was pinch'd, and pull'd she said,
And he by friar's lanthorn led
Tells how the drudging goblin sweat,   105
To earn his cream-bowl duly set,
When in one night, ere glimpse of morn,
His shadowy flail hath thresh'd the corn
That ten day-labourers could not end,
Then lies him down the lubber fiend,   110
And stretch'd out all the chimney's length,
Basks at the fire his hairy strength;
And crop-full out of doors he flings,
Ere the first cock his matin rings.
Thus done the tales, to bed they creep,   115
By whispering winds soon lull'd asleep.
Tow'red cities please us then,
And the busy hum of men,
Where throngs of knights and barons bold,
In weeds of peace high triumphs hold,   120
With store of ladies, whose bright eyes

132 sock the light shoe of ancient comic actors, a symbol of comedy
133–4 Shakespeare is characterised partly in contrast with the learned Jonson (cf. *On Shakespeare* 9–10), partly in terms of the outdoor comedies the mirthful man would enjoy.
135 eating cares cf. Horace, *Od.* 2.11.18
136 Lydian sensuous, relaxing (the young Milton is less severe than Plato, *Rep.* 398–9)
136–7 Cf. Horace, *Od.* 4.15.30
136–44 Since Milton links music with song he seems to be thinking, not so much of the unaccompanied madrigal or part-song, but of the solo 'air' or Italian aria.
139 bout turn, involution

Rain influence, and judge the prize
Of wit, or arms, while both contend
To win her grace, whom all commend.
There let Hymen oft appear   125
In saffron robe, with taper clear,
And pomp, and feast, and revelry,
With mask, and antique pageantry,
Such sights as youthful poets dream
On summer eves by haunted stream.   130
Then to the well-trod stage anon,
If Jonson's learned sock be on,
Or sweetest Shakespeare fancy's child,
Warble his native wood-notes wild,
And ever against eating cares,   135
Lap me in soft Lydian airs,
Married to immortal verse
Such as the meeting soul may pierce
In notes, with many a winding bout
Of linked sweetness long drawn out,   140
With wanton heed, and giddy cunning,
The melting voice through mazes running;
Untwisting all the chains that tie
The hidden soul of harmony.
That Orpheus' self may heave his head   145
From golden slumber on a bed
Of heap'd Elysian flow'rs, and hear
Such strains as would have won the ear
Of Pluto, to have quite set free
His half-regain'd Eurydice.   150
These delights, if thou canst give,
Mirth with thee I mean to live.

                          (1631–2?)

1–10 The vain joys here dismissed are empty levity, not the refined Mirth celebrated in *L'Allegro*.

8 Cf. Chaucer *Wife of Bath's Tale* 868

10 **pensioners** attendants **Morpheus** god of dreams

12–16 **Melancholy** means literally 'black bile,' one of the four humours. The 'black' or darkened skin associated with this Milton links with the benign kind of melancholy that accompanied genius and philosophical and poetical contemplation.
18 **Memnon** a handsome Ethiopian prince who fought in the Trojan War
19–21 Like a number of other writers, Milton has Cassiopeia boast of her own beauty, not that of her daughter Andromeda; she was made a constellation.
23 **Vesta**, the Roman goddess of the hearth adds the idea of the purity of celestial fire.
24 f. **Saturn** son of Heaven and Earth; rebelled against Ophion, the ruler of Olympus, and reigned himself, creating a golden age

Il Penseroso

Hence vain deluding Joys,
   The brood of Folly without father bred,
How little you bestead,
   Or fill the fixed mind with all your toys;
Dwell in some idle brain,   5
   And fancies fond with gaudy shapes possess,
As thick and numberless
   As the gay motes that people the sunbeams,
Or likest hovering dreams
   The fickle pensioners of Morpheus' train.   10

But hail thou goddess, sage and holy,
Hail divinest Melancholy,
Whose saintly visage is too bright
To hit the sense of human sight;
And therefore to our weaker view,   15
O'erlaid with black staid wisdom's hue.
Black, but such as in esteem,
Prince Memnon's sister might beseem,
Or that starr'd Ethiop queen that strove
To set her beauty's praise above   20
The sea-nymphs, and their powers offended.
Yet thou art higher far descended,
Thee bright-hair'd Vesta long of yore,
To solitary Saturn bore;
His daughter she (in Saturn's reign,   25
Such mixture was not held a stain)
Oft in glimmering bow'rs, and glades

30 Jove Zeus (Jupiter), who was brought up on Mount Ida in Crete, later overthrew his father Cronos (Saturn).

37 Cf. Jonson, *Queen and huntress* 4: 'State in wonted manner keep'

39 Cf. Ovid, *Ars Amatoria* 3.549, 'commercia caeli'

42 Cf. *On Shakespeare* 14
43 leaden In alchemy Saturn is associated with lead.

52–4 Ezek. 1 and 10

55 hist summon with the quiet exclamation 'hist'

He met her, and in secret shades
Of woody Ida's inmost grove,
While yet there was no fear of Jove.   30
Come pensive nun, devout and pure,
Sober, steadfast, and demure,
All in a robe of darkest grain,
Flowing with majestic train,
And sable stole of cypress lawn,   35
Over thy decent shoulders drawn.
Come, but keep thy wonted state,
With ev'n step, and musing gate,
And looks commercing with the skies,
Thy rapt soul sitting in thine eyes: 40
There held in holy passion still,
Forget thyself to marble, till
With a sad leaden downward cast,
Thou fix them on the earth as fast.
And join with thee calm Peace, and Quiet,   45
Spare Fast, that oft with gods doth diet,
And hears the Muses in a ring,
Ay round about Jove's altar sing.
And add to these retired Leisure,
That in trim gardens takes his pleasure;   50
But first, and chiefest, with thee bring
Him that yon soars on golden wing,
Guiding the fiery-wheeled throne,
The cherub Contemplation,
And the mute Silence hist along,   55
'Less Philomel will deign a song,
In her sweetest, saddest plight,
Smoothing the rugged brow of night,

59   Cynthia (the moon) is given the dragon-chariot associated with Hecate, the goddess in her underworld aspect.

83   bellman the night-watchman calling the hours

87 That is, stay up all night, since the Great Bear does not set
88 Hermes 'Trismegistus': supposed author of neoplatonic books written at Alexandria in the 2nd and 3rd centuries A.D., which, translated by the Florentine Platonist Marsilio Ficino, had much influence   **unsphere** call back

While Cynthia checks her dragon yoke,
Gently o'er th' accustom'd oak;   60
Sweet bird that shunn'st the noise of folly,
Most musical, most melancholy!
Thee chauntress oft the woods among,
I woo to hear thy even-song;
And missing thee, I walk unseen   65
On the dry smooth-shaven green,
To behold the wand'ring moon,
Riding near her highest noon,
Like one that had been led astray
Through the heav'n's wide pathless way;   70
And oft, as if her head she bow'd,
Stooping through a fleecy cloud.
Oft on a plat of rising ground,
I hear the far-off curfew sound,
Over some wide-water'd shore,   75
Swinging slow with sullen roar;
Or if the air will not permit,
Some still removed place will fit,
Where glowing embers through the room
Teach light to counterfeit a gloom,   80
Far from all resort of mirth,
Save the cricket on the hearth,
Or the bellman's drowsy charm,
To bless the doors from nightly harm:
Or let my lamp at midnight hour,   85
Be seen in some high lonely tow'r,
Where I may oft out-watch the Bear,
With thrice great Hermes, or unsphere
The spirit of Plato to unfold

93-6   The four elements, earth, water, air, fire, were associated with various orders of spirits.

98   pall robe

99   Thebes tragedies concerning Oedipus and his family   **Pelops' line** Pelops was the ancestor of Atreus and Thyestes, Agamemnon, Orestes, Electra, and Iphigenia.

102   The buskin, a high shoe worn by ancient tragic actors, corresponds to the 'sock' of *L'Allegro* 132.

104   Musaeus a mythical Greek poet

108   Pluto's conditional release of Eurydice (*L'Allegro* 145 f.)

109-15   Chaucer's unfinished *Squire's Tale*

116-20   Chiefly, no doubt, *The Faerie Queene*, by 'our sage and serious poet Spenser' (*Areopagitica*, *Works*, 4, 311); also, Tasso's *Gerusalemme Liberata* and parts of Ariosto's *Orlando Furioso*

What worlds, or what vast regions hold   90
Th' immortal mind that hath forsook
Her mansion in this fleshly nook:
And of those demons that are found
In fire, air, flood, or under ground,
Whose power hath a true consent   95
With planet, or with element.
Sometime let gorgeous Tragedy
In sceptred pall come sweeping by,
Presenting Thebes, or Pelops' line,
Or the tale of Troy divine,   100
Or what (though rare) of later age,
Ennobled hath the buskin'd stage.
But, O sad virgin, that thy power
Might raise Musaeus from his bower,
Or bid the soul of Orpheus sing   105
Such notes as warbled to the string,
Drew iron tears down Pluto's cheek,
And made hell grant what love did seek.
Or call up him that left half told
The story of Cambuscan bold,   110
Of Camball, and of Algarsife,
And who had Canace to wife,
That own'd the virtuous ring and glass,
And of the wondrous horse of brass,
On which the Tartar king did ride;   115
And if aught else, great bards beside,
In sage and solemn tunes have sung,
Of tourneys and of trophies hung;
Of forests, and enchantments drear,
Where more is meant than meets the ear.   120

122   civil-suited plainly dressed (cf. *Romeo and Juliet* 3.2.10–11)   **frounc'd**
with hair curled

124   Attic boy Cephalus, the hunter loved by Aurora

126   rocking winds that cause to rock (Sandys used 'rocking winds' in
translating Ovid, *Met.* 7.585–86)

130   minute drops drops falling at intervals of a minute

141   Cf. 'garish sun,' *Romeo and Juliet* 3.2.25

144–6   Cf. Horace, *Epod.* 2.27–8

148–50   Wave . . . laid come floating with the wings of Sleep as they settle
on my eyes

Thus night oft see me in thy pale career,
Till civil-suited morn appear,
Not trick'd and frounc'd as she was wont,
With the Attic boy to hunt,
But kerchieft in a com'ly cloud,   125
While rocking winds are piping loud,
Or usher'd with a shower still,
When the gust hath blown his fill,
Ending on the rustling leaves,
With minute drops from off the eaves.   130
And when the sun begins to fling
His flaring beams, me goddess bring
To arched walks of twilight groves,
And shadows brown that Sylvan loves
Of pine, or monumental oak,   135
Where the rude axe with heaved stroke,
Was never heard the nymphs to daunt,
Or fright them from their hallow'd haunt.
There in close covert by some brook,
Where no profaner eye may look,   140
Hide me from day's garish eye,
While the bee with honied thigh,
That at her flow'ry work doth sing,
And the waters murmuring
With such consort as they keep,   145
Entice the dewy-feather'd Sleep;
And let some strange mysterious dream
Wave at his wings in airy stream,
Of lively portraiture display'd,
Softly on my eyelids laid.   150
And as I wake, sweet music breathe

156   pale enclosure

157   embowed vaulted

160   Cf. More's *Utopia*, tr. R. Robinson (Everyman's Library, pp. 107–08): 'Because they thought that overmuch light doth disperse men's cogitations whereas in dim and doubtful light they be gathered together, and more earnestly fixed upon religion and devotion'

170–71   spell Of interpret

Above, about, or underneath,
Sent by some spirit to mortals good,
Or th' unseen genius of the wood.
But let my due feet never fail   155
To walk the studious cloister's pale,
And love the high embowed roof,
With antique pillars' massy proof,
And storied windows richly dight,
Casting a dim religious light.   160
There let the pealing organ blow
To the full-voic'd choir below,
In service high, and anthems clear,
As may with sweetness, through mine ear,
Dissolve me into ecstasies,   165
And bring all heav'n before mine eyes.
And may at last my weary age
Find out the peaceful hermitage,
The hairy gown and mossy cell,
Where I may sit and rightly spell   170
Of every star that heav'n doth shew,
And every herb that sips the dew;
Till old experience do attain
To something like prophetic strain.
These pleasures Melancholy give,   175
And I with thee will choose to live.
                    (1631–2?)

Arcades dwellers in Arcadia, a region in southern Greece; the ideal pastoral world

Arcades

The Countess Dowager of Derby was the widow of Queen Elizabeth's Lord Keeper, Sir Thomas Egerton, later Lord Ellesmere (who had had John Donne as his secretary), but she was known by the title that came from her first husband; to go back further, she was one of the three daughters of Sir John Spencer who had received dedications from their kinsman, Edmund Spenser. Her home, Harefield, was some ten miles from Horton (the Miltons may not have been living there yet). It is almost certain that the performance was managed by the court musician, Henry Lawes, who later produced *Comus*; he was musical tutor in the family of the Countess' stepson, the Earl of Bridgewater, and was probably, through his music, an old acquaintance of the elder Milton, a composer, and his poet-son. *Arcades* is the first work transcribed in the manuscript (preserved at Trinity College, Cambridge) in which Milton began to copy his poems; but that fact does not help much to narrow down the conjectural date, 1630–34. The Countess became 70 about 1630 and that or another birthday might have furnished the occasion. It seems unlikely that, after the solemn self-dedication of Sonnet VII (probably December 9, 1632), Milton would soon have written a mainly secular piece (even though it includes a passage of exalted and quasi-religious Platonism). A closer guess might be the spring or summer of 1632. When asked to supply such a script, Milton would no doubt have reviewed Ben Jonson, and *Arcades* seems to show marks of imitation, both in the lyrics and in the figure and speech of the Genius. It is a courtly and graceful miniature, pastoral and mythological.

Part of an entertainment presented to the Countess Dowager of Derby at Harefield, by some noble persons of her family, who

12   Cf. 1 Kings 10.7

20   **Latona** mother of Apollo and Diana

21   **Cybele** wife of Cronos, mother of the gods; she wore a turreted head-dress

23   **Juno** wife of Jupiter and queen of the gods

appear on the scene in pastoral habit, moving toward the seat of state, with this song.

1. Song

Look nymphs, and shepherds look,
What sudden blaze of majesty
Is that which we from hence descry
Too divine to be mistook:
   This this is she   5
To whom our vows and wishes bend,
Here our solemn search hath end.

Fame that her high worth to raise
Seem'd erst so lavish and profuse,
We may justly now accuse   10
Of detraction from her praise,
   Less than half we find express'd,
   Envy bid conceal the rest.

Mark what radiant state she spreads
In circle round her shining throne,   15
Shooting her beams like silver threads.
This this is she alone,
   Sitting like a goddess bright
   In the centre of her light.

Might she the wise Latona be   20
Or the tow'red Cybele,
Mother of a hundred gods;
Juno dares not give her odds;

Genius local divinity (*Nativity* 186; *Il Penseroso* 154; *Lycidas* 183)

27   honour noble descent (cf. 'gentle', **2**6)

46   curl adorn (cf. Jonson, *To Sir Robert Wroth* 17, 'the curled woods')

Who had thought this clime had held
A deity so unparallel'd?   25

*As they come forward, the Genius of the Wood appears, and turning
toward them, speaks.*

Gen. Stay gentle swains, for though in this disguise,
I see bright honour sparkle through your eyes.
Of famous Arcady ye are, and sprung
Of that renowned flood so often sung,
Divine Alphéus, who by secret sluice,   30
Stole under seas to meet his Arethuse;
And ye the breathing roses of the wood,
Fair silver-buskin'd nymphs as great and good,
I know this quest of yours, and free intent
Was all in honour and devotion meant   35
To the great mistress of yon princely shrine,
Whom with low reverence I adore as mine,
And with all helpful service will comply
To further this night's glad solemnity;
And lead ye where ye may more near behold   40
What shallow-searching Fame hath left untold;
Which I full oft amidst these shades alone
Have sat to wonder at, and gaze upon:
For know by lot from Jove I am the pow'r
Of this fair wood, and live in oak'n bow'r,   45
To nurse the saplings tall, and curl the grove
With ringlets quaint, and wanton windings wove.
And all my plants I save from nightly ill
Of noisome winds, or blasting vapours chill,
And from the boughs brush off the evil dew,   50

52   cross . . . planet malign Saturn (cf. *Epitaphium Damonis* 80)

63 f.   Not the Homeric Sirens but those described in Plato's myth of Er (*Rep.* 616–17), the angelic intelligences who attend the celestial spheres; these turn on a spindle which rests on the knees of Necessity, mother of the three Fates

72–3   Cf. *Nativity* 125 f. and note

And heal the harms of thwarting thunder blue
Or what the cross dire-looking planet smites,
Or hurtful worm with canker'd venom bites.
When ev'ning grey doth rise, I fetch my round
Over the mount, and all this hallow'd ground,   55
And early ere the odorous breath of morn
Awakes the slumb'ring leaves, or tassel'd horn
Shakes the high thicket, haste I all about,
Number my ranks, and visit every sprout
With puissant words, and murmurs made to bless,   60
But else in deep of night when drowsiness
Hath lock'd up mortal sense, then listen I
To the celestial sirens' harmony,
That sit upon the nine enfolded spheres,
And sing to those that hold the vital shears,   65
And turn the adamantine spindle round,
On which the fate of gods and men is wound.
Such sweet compulsion doth in music lie,
To lull the daughters of Necessity
And keep unsteady nature to her law,   70
And the low world in measur'd motion draw
After the heav'nly tune, which none can hear
Of human mould with gross unpurged ear;
And yet such music worthiest were to blaze
The peerless height of her immortal praise,   75
Whose lustre leads us, and for her most fit,
If my inferior hand or voice could hit
Inimitable sounds, yet as we go,
Whate'er the skill of lesser gods can show,
I will assay, her worth to celebrate,   80
And so attend ye toward her glittering state;

82 stem family

89 Cf. Spenser, *F.Q.* 1.1.7.6

97 Ladon a river in Arcadia
98–102 Names of Arcadian mountains associated mainly with Pan

Where ye may all that are of noble stem
Approach, and kiss her sacred vesture's hem.

2. Song

O'er the smooth enamell'd green
Where no print of step hath been,   85
   Follow me as I sing,
   And touch the warbled string.
Under the shady roof
Of branching elm star-proof,   90
   Follow me;
I will bring you where she sits,
Clad in splendour as befits
   Her deity.
   Such a rural queen
All Arcadia hath not seen.   95

3. Song

   Nymphs and shepherds dance no more
   By sandy Ladon's lilied banks.
On old Lycaeus or Cyllene hoar,
   Trip no more in twilight ranks,
Though Erymanth your loss deplore,   100
   A better soil shall give ye thanks.
From the stony Maenalus
Bring your flocks, and live with us.
   Here ye shall have greater grace
   To serve the Lady of this place.   105

Though Syrinx your Pan's mistress were,
Yet Syrinx well might wait on her.
   Such a rural queen
All Arcadia hath not seen.

                 (1632?)

2   Milton apparently means 'my first 23 years'.

Sonnet VII

This sonnet seems to have been written on Milton's twenty-fourth birthday (December 9, 1632) not on his twenty-third. (Titles containing the words 'age of twenty-three' and the like are late editorial additions and have no authority.) The date is important in regard to Milton's state of mind. He had become a literary and intellectual figure in the Cambridge world, but now he has been for six months an obscure student under his father's roof, beginning the years of hard reading by which he hoped to prepare himself for the unknown future; meanwhile his contemporaries are forging ahead. This religious self-dedication is a landmark in Milton's early development; the poems that followed it appear (though some dates are uncertain) to have been all more or less religious. In a letter written early in 1633 to a friend (perhaps his old tutor, Thomas Young), who had warned him against indulgence in study and urged an active life, presumably in the ministry, Milton replied with an account of his earnest reflections. Having in mind the parables of the talents and the vineyard, he still thinks he should not be anxious about 'being late, so it gives advantage to be more fit.' But he included a copy of the sonnet as proof 'that I am something suspicious of myself, and do take notice of a certain belatedness in me.'

Compared with most of the later sonnets, this one is strictly regular in its formal divisions; and the sestet, though deeply charged with feeling, is plain, unfigurative statement.

How soon hath time the subtle thief of youth,
    Stolen on his wing my three and twentieth year!
    My hasting days fly on with full career,
    But my late spring no bud or blossom shew'th.
Perhaps my semblance might deceive the truth   5

8   Among contemporaries who might have been in Milton's mind was his friend and junior, Diodati.

9–14   Milton may be giving a Christian turn to lines 41–43 of Pindar's fourth Nemean ode: 'But whatever excellence Lord Destiny gave me, well I know that creeping time will bring its appointed fulfilment.'

13   All is, if i.e. all depends on whether

That I to manhood am arriv'd so near,
And inward ripeness doth much less appear,
That some more timely-happy spirits endu'th.
Yet be it less or more, or soon or slow,
  It shall be still in strictest measure ev'n   10
  To that same lot, however mean or high,
Toward which time leads me, and the will of heav'n;
  All is, if I have grace to use it so,
  As ever in my great task-master's eye.

                    (December 9, 1632?)

12 A kiss given to every individual soul; or perhaps 'undividable,' 'eternal'

14 **sincerely** purely, wholly

On Time

This and the next two poems form a group which apparently followed close upon Sonnet VII. Milton's gambit in the first one is explained by the subtitle in the Cambridge manuscript, 'To be set on a clock case'. In most Renaissance poets the idea of time inspired neo-pagan and amatory variations, gay or sober, on the Horatian text *carpe diem*, though some could sound a religious note. Milton is wholly religious in his contrast between earthly flux and sin and the eternal purity and joy of the soul's life in heaven. The form, a paragraph with lines of irregular length and irregular rhymes, is that of an Italian madrigal; the slow movement, the manipulation of phrase and rhythm, gives full weight to every word.

Fly envious Time, till thou run out thy race,
Call on the lazy leaden-stepping hours,
Whose speed is but the heavy plummet's pace;
And glut thyself with what thy womb devours,
Which is no more than what is false and vain,   5
And merely mortal dross;
So little is our loss,
So little is thy gain.
For when as each thing bad thou hast entomb'd,
And last of all thy greedy self consum'd,   10
Then long eternity shall greet our bliss
With an individual kiss;
And joy shall overtake us as a flood,
When every thing that is sincerely good
And perfectly divine,   15
With truth, and peace, and love shall ever shine
About the supreme throne

18   happy-making sight 'the beatific vision' (cf. *P.L.* 1.684, 3.61–62)

21   Attir'd with stars like figures of pagan myth changed into constellations; also, in old tradition the stars were of ethereal, indestructible substance

Of him t' whose happy-making sight alone,
When once our heav'nly-guided soul shall climb,
Then all this earthy grossness quit,   20
Attir'd with stars, we shall for ever sit,
   Triumphing over death, and chance, and thee O Time.

(1632?)

1   powers cf. *Nativity* 112–13 and note

10   whilere lately

17–20   Cf. *Nativity* 1–14 and notes

Upon the Circumcision

Since the circumcision of the infant Jesus is commemorated on January 1, Milton presumably wrote this poem on or about that day, 1633. His choice of a theme may have been prompted more by the church calendar than by authentic inspiration, since the poem flags after the opening lines. The stanza form is close to that of Petrarch's canzone to the Blessed Virgin (*Vergine bella, che di Sol vestita*) and that of Tasso's *Alla Beatissima Vergine in Loreto*.

  Ye flaming powers, and winged warriors bright
That erst with music, and triumphant song
First heard by happy watchful shepherd's ear,
So sweetly sung your joy the clouds along
Through the soft silence of the list'ning night,   5
Now mourn, and if sad share with us to bear
Your fiery essence can distil no tear,
Burn in your sighs, and borrow
Seas wept from our deep sorrow.
He who with all heav'n's heraldry whilere   10
Enter'd the world, now bleeds to give us ease;
Alas, how soon our sin
    Sore doth begin
His infancy to seize!
  O more exceeding love or law more just?   15
Just law indeed, but more exceeding love!
For we by rightful doom remediless
Were lost in death till he that dwelt above
High-thron'd in secret bliss, for us frail dust
Emptied his glory, ev'n to nakedness;   20

21 cov'nant The covenant of grace, first adumbrated in Gen. 3.15 and fulfilled in redemption through Christ, superseded the Mosaic law of works.

And that great cov'nant which we still transgress
Entirely satisfi'd,
And the full wrath beside
Of vengeful justice bore for our excess,
And seals obedience first with wounding smart   25
This day, but O ere long
    Huge pangs and strong
Will pierce more near his heart.

                  (1633?)

The title means 'At a Concert of Sacred Music'.
1–2 Voice and Verse are the earthly counterparts of the Platonic Sirens of *Arcades* 63 f.

5 phantasy imagination

6 consent harmony

7–16 Ezek. 1.26, Rev. 7.9–15

14 just spirits the redeemed (cf. *Comus* 9–11)

18 noise cf. Ps. 100.1, 'Make a joyful noise unto the Lord'

At a Solemn Music

This poem was probably written early in 1633. The Cambridge manuscript has two drafts and a fair copy. Milton takes up again the double
theme of *On Time*, but in reverse order: here he moves from the
harmony of heaven down to the sinful discords of earth, though the
last lines return to the celestial vision. Obviously the whole poem
works out a musical metaphor. As in *On Time*, the irregular lines and
slow movement elicit full and fresh value from even the most ordinary words. The first 24 lines constitute a single sentence.

Blest pair of Sirens, pledges of heav'n's joy,
Sphere-born, harmonious sisters, Voice, and Verse,
Wed your divine sounds, and mixed power employ
Dead things with inbreath'd sense able to pierce
And to our high-rais'd phantasy present   5
That undisturbed song of pure consent
Ay sung before the sapphire-colour'd throne
To him that sits thereon
With saintly shout, and solemn jubilee,
Where the bright seraphim in burning row   10
Their loud up-lifted angel trumpets blow,
And the cherubic host in thousand choirs
Touch their immortal harps of golden wires
With those just spirits that wear victorious palms,
Hymns devout and holy psalms   15
Singing everlastingly;
That we on earth with undiscording voice
May rightly answer that melodious noise
As once we did, till disproportion'd sin

23 diapason concord

Jarr'd against nature's chime, and with harsh din   20
Broke the fair music that all creatures made
To their great Lord, whose love their motion sway'd
In perfect diapason, whilst they stood
In first obedience, and their state of good.
O may we soon again renew that song,   25
And keep in tune with heav'n, till God ere long
To his celestial consort us unite
    To live with him, and sing in endless morn of light.
                        (1633?)

A Mask
Presented at Ludlow Castle
[*Comus*]

The quality of *Arcades* led Henry Lawes to turn again to Milton with a larger commission, the writing of a masque for the inauguration of the Earl of Bridgewater as Lord President of Wales. To the young poet, who was pursuing his private studies at home and had not written anything for some time, the invitation provided no doubt an agreeable interlude. His 'Mask'—the handy but illogical title *Comus* was first adopted in the eighteenth century for stage performances—was presented at Ludlow Castle in Shropshire on September 29, 1634. Lawes, the producer and composer of music for the songs, took the role of the Attendant Spirit. The parts of the Elder and Second Brother and the Lady were acted by the Earl's children, Viscount Brackley and Thomas and Lady Alice Egerton, who, though only eleven, nine, and fifteen respectively, had already appeared in masques at court.

From the accession of King James in 1603 up to 1640, two years before the outbreak of the civil war, masques were a favourite form of entertainment at court and sometimes at noble houses. The masque gained artistic status especially through the partnership of Ben Jonson and the great stage designer and architect, Inigo Jones, and the genre attracted many other poets and dramatists from Samuel Daniel and Thomas Campion to Thomas Carew and James Shirley. As a rule the masque did not attempt to be dramatic; the libretto, allegorical or mythological or both, might touch a serious theme, but it was mainly an excuse for an abundance of spectacle, music, and dancing. Court productions were lavish and expensive.

Arcades, though a miniature, was closer to the standard type than *Comus*, which developed a moral and religious theme through a semi-dramatic story and elaborate and weighty speeches. The acting version, however, was somewhat shorter than the one we read: it did not contain the Lady's most impassioned reply to Comus and some other passages (lines 195–225, 737–55, 779–806, 997, 1000–1011), which appeared in the text published by Lawes in 1637 and in that of Milton's *Poems* (1645). Also, the Attendant Spirit's epilogue was, in shorter form, a prologue. Up to a point Milton followed the conventions: he furnished a modicum of spectacle, singing, and dancing, and, in Comus and his beast-headed crew, he exploited the 'antimasque', the grotesque feature often contrasted with the ordered beauty of the whole. But in its treatment of a serious subject, and in the texture of the poetry, *Comus* was far above the normal masque— and very far above the spurious 'Platonics' in vogue at the Caroline court. The masque was soon in demand for reading and Lawes had so many requests for copies that in 1637 he printed it, evidently with Milton's consent, though he withheld his name.

Many 'sources' have been suggested as contributing to Milton's plot or theme or pastoral atmosphere: George Peele's *Old Wives' Tale*, John Fletcher's *Faithful Shepherdess*, the Latin fable *Comus* (1608) by the Dutch Erycius Puteanus; *The Tempest*; William Browne's *Inner Temple Masque* (1615), on the myth of Circe, and Jonson's *Pleasure Reconciled to Virtue* (1618), in which Comus appeared as a crude belly-god (neither of these masques was in print in 1634); another masque of Jonson's, *Hymenaei* (printed in 1606 and 1616); and Tasso's famous pastoral play, *Aminta*, and an Italian musical drama, *La Catena d'Adone* (1626). But, whether or not Milton knew some or all of these works, they would be far less important than Homer and Ovid and Spenser. Homer's tale of Odysseus and Circe was for the Renaissance the great *exemplum* of heroic virtue confronted by sensual temptation, and it was elaborately reworked by such major poets as Ariosto, Tasso, and Spenser. (Milton, in his first rendering of the conflict between good and evil, gave the story a fresh turn by making Comus the son of Circe and the inheritor of her magical powers.) Spenser had used the idea in book two of *The Faerie Queene*, the book of temperance, and in his third book he had the parallel episode of the virtuous Amoret held captive by the sensual Busyrane. Spenser was Milton's great predecessor in the poetic and figurative treatment of moral and religious ideas, and in *Areopagitica* Milton was to refer to the Cave of Mammon and the Bower of Bliss devised by 'our sage and serious poet Spenser, whom I dare be known to think a better teacher than Scotus or Aquinas.'

The allegorical interpretation of the Homeric tale was a universal commonplace—Milton alluded to it at the end of his first Latin elegy—and it was fully set forth in the commentary that George Sandys in 1632 added to his translation of Ovid's *Metamorphoses*. Whether or not Milton had looked into the book—and such a lover of Ovid may well have done so—some of Sandys' phrases are suggestive. Ulysses, 'being fortified by an immortal power, was not subject to mutation. For the divine and celestial soul, subsisting through the bounty of the Creator, can by no assault of nature be violated, nor can that be converted into a beast which so highly participates of reason. . . .' Circe's allurements cannot be resisted 'but by the divine assistance, Moly, the gift of Mercury, which signifies temperance. . . .' Men whose appetites 'revolt from the sovereignty of reason (by which we are only like unto God, and armed against depraved affections)' can never 'return into their country (from whence the soul deriveth her celestial original) unless disenchanted and cleansed from their former impurity.'

The Platonic colouring of Sandys' comments brings us to what is by far the best of all introductions to *Comus* and to much of Milton's earlier poetry, his own account, in *An Apology for Smectymnuus* (1642), of the growth of his youthful ideal of chastity and the reading that fostered it. The all-important passage needs to be read and reread:

> . . . I had my time, readers, as others have, who have good learning bestowed upon them, to be sent to those places where, the opinion was, it might be soonest attained; and as the manner is, was not unstudied in those authors which are most commended;

whereof some were grave orators and historians, whose matter methought I loved indeed, but as my age then was, so I understood them; others were the smooth elegiac poets,[1] whereof the schools are not scarce, whom both for the pleasing sound of their numerous[2] writing, which in imitation I found most easy, and most agreeable to nature's part in me, and for their matter, which what it is, there be few who know not, I was so allured to read, that no recreation came to me better welcome. For that it was then those years with me which are excused, though they be least severe, I may be saved the labour to remember ye. Whence having observed them to account it the chief glory of their wit, in that they were ablest to judge, to praise, and by that could esteem themselves worthiest to love those high perfections, which under one or other name they took to celebrate; I thought with myself by every instinct and presage of nature, which is not wont to be false, that what emboldened them to this task, might with such diligence as they used embolden me; and that what judgement, wit, or elegance was my share, would herein best appear, and best value itself, by how much more wisely and with more love of virtue I should choose (let rude ears be absent) the object of not unlike praises. For albeit these thought to some will seem virtuous and commendable, to others only pardonable, to a third sort perhaps idle; yet the mentioning of them now will end in serious. Nor blame it, readers, in those years to propose to themselves such a reward, as the noblest dispositions above other things in this life have sometimes preferred; whereof not to be sensible when good and fair in one person meet, argues both a gross and shallow judgement, and withal an ungentle and swainish breast. For by the firm settling of these persuasions, I became, to my best memory, so much a proficient, that if I found

---

[1] Ovid, Propertius, and Tibullus, whose love-poems were written in elegiac metre
[2] **numerous** metrical, rhythmical

those authors[1] anywhere speaking unworthy things of themselves, or unchaste of those names which before they had extolled, this effect it wrought with me, from that time forward their art I still applauded, but the men I deplored; and above them all, preferred the two famous renowners of Beatrice and Laura,[2] who never write but honour of them to whom they devote their verse, displaying sublime and pure thoughts, without transgression. And long it was not after, when I was confirmed in this opinion, that he who would not be frustrate of his hope to write well hereafter in laudable things, ought himself to be a true poem; that is, a composition and pattern of the best and honourablest things;[3] not presuming to sing high praises of heroic men, or famous cities, unless he have in himself the experience and the practice of all that which is praiseworthy. These reasonings, together with a certain niceness[4] of nature, an honest haughtiness, and self-esteem either of what I was, or what I might be (which let envy call pride), and lastly that modesty, whereof, though not in the title-page, yet here I may be excused to make some beseeming profession; all these uniting the supply of their natural aid together, kept me still above those low descents of mind, beneath which he must deject and plunge himself, that can agree to saleable and unlawful prostitutions. Next (for hear me out now, readers), that I may tell ye whither my younger feet wandered; I betook me among those lofty fables and romances which recount in solemn cantos the deeds of knighthood founded by our victorious kings, and from hence had in renown over all Christendom. There I read it in the oath of every knight, that he should defend to the expense of his best blood, or of his life, if it so befell him, the honour and chastity of virgin or matron; from whence even then I learned what a

---

[1] **authors** Ovid and other love-poets
[2] The women celebrated by Dante and Petrarch
[3] A classical ideal revived by Renaissance poets; cf. Jonson's dedication of *Volpone*
[4] **niceness** fastidiousness

noble virtue chastity sure must be, to the defence of which so many worthies, by such a dear adventure of themselves, had sworn. And if I found in the story afterward, any of them, by word or deed, breaking that oath, I judged it the same fault of the poet as that which is attributed to Homer, to have written indecent things of the gods. Only this my mind gave me, that every free and gentle spirit, without that oath, ought to be born a knight, nor needed to expect the gilt spur, or the laying of a sword upon his shoulder to stir him up both by his counsel and his arms, to secure and protect the weakness of any attempted[1] chastity. So that even these books, which to many others have been the fuel of wantonness and loose living, I cannot think how, unless by divine indulgence, proved to me so many incitements, as you have heard, to the love and steadfast observation of that virtue which abhors the society of bordelloes. Thus, from the laureat fraternity of poets, riper years and the ceaseless round of study and reading led me to the shady spaces of philosophy, but chiefly to the divine volumes of Plato, and his equal[2] Xeno-phon; where, if I should tell ye what I learnt of chastity and love, I mean that which is truly so, whose charming cup is only virtue, which she bears in her hand to those who are worthy (the rest are cheated with a thick, intoxicating potion, which a certain sorceress,[3] the abuser of love's name, carries about); and how the first and chiefest office of love begins and ends in the soul, producing those happy twins of her divine generation, knowledge and virtue. With such abstracted sublimities as these, it might be worth your listening, readers, as I may one day hope to have ye in a still time, when there shall be no chiding; not in these noises, the adversary, as ye know, barking at the door, or searching for me at the bordelloes, where it may be he had lost himself, and raps up without pity the sage and

[1] **attempted** attacked
[2] **equal** contemporary
[3] **sorceress** Circe

rheumatic old prelatess with all her young Corinthian laity[1],
to inquire for such a one. Last of all, not in time, but as perfection
is last, that care was ever had of me, with my earliest capacity,
not to be negligently trained in the precepts of the Christian
religion: this that I have hitherto related, hath been to show,
that though Christianity had been but slightly taught me, yet a
certain reservedness of natural disposition, and moral discipline,
learnt out of the noblest philosophy, was enough to keep me in
disdain of far less incontinences than this of the bordello. But
having had the doctrine of holy scripture unfolding those chaste
and high mysteries with timeliest care infused, that 'the body is
for the Lord, and the Lord for the body';[2] thus also I argued to
myself that if unchastity in a woman, whom St Paul terms the
glory of man,[3] be such a scandal and dishonour, then certainly in
a man, who is both the image and glory of God, it must, though
commonly not so thought, be much more deflouring and dis-
honourable, in that he sins both against his own body, which is
the perfecter sex, and his own glory, which is in the woman and,
that which is worst, against the image and glory of God, which
is in himself. Nor did I slumber over that place[4] expressing such
high rewards of ever accompanying the Lamb with those celestial
songs to others inapprehensible, but not to those who were not
defiled with women, which doubtless means fornication, for
marriage must not be called a defilement. Thus large I have pur-
posely been, that if I have been justly taxed with this crime,
it may come upon me, after all this my confession, with a tenfold
shame.

Thus *Comus* is not a mere negative exposition of chastity as abstinence from vice but a positive and all-embracing celebration of the

[1] **laity** prostitutes
[2] 1 Cor. 6.13
[3] 1 Cor. 11.7
[4] **place** passage (Rev. 14.3–4)

Platonic and Christian love of the good. Like all Christian humanists, Milton sees the highest pagan ethics, with the special inspiration of Platonic love, as a strong ally of Christian ethics, and he recognises both the difference between them and their necessary fusion. The Second Brother is immature and anxious. The confident Elder Brother, somewhat in the manner of a contemporary student delivering academic speeches, appeals less to religious faith than to classical reason. The Lady represents a mature blending of the two. Sabrina, who is invoked to free the Lady, may stand for the divine grace that must reinforce rational temperance. The Attendant Spirit is a Neoplatonic daemon who has the virtually Christian function of a guardian angel. The first paragraph of his opening speech renews the theme of *On Time* and *At a Solemn Music*, the contrast between heaven (here a Platonic-Christian heaven) and sinworn earth; and his epilogue is a religious benediction upon the victory won, a religious injunction to love the true freedom of goodness.

Comus, it may be added, is a gentleman of cultivated sensibility; his inward corruption is shown—as Satan's is to be, on a grand scale —by the ironic method of self-revelation. His central speech to the Lady on Nature's bounties (706 f.) is a unique piece of writing; its vivid, sprawling immediacy of tactual and visual images has the effect of betraying the speaker's moral disorder.

Most of *Comus* is written in blank verse—Milton's first venture in that medium—and it varies in movement from the smooth and semilyrical to the irregular and colloquial. In point of style, the masque may almost be called a mosaic of different styles, which range from Elizabethan pastoralism to Augustan classicism, though every line bears the stamp of its author. One must quote the famous eulogy included in the letter of advice on travel which Sir Henry Wotton sent to Milton in April, 1638, and which was prefixed to *Comus* in the *Poems* of 1645: 'Wherein I should much commend the tragical part, if the lyrical did not ravish me with a certain Doric delicacy in your songs and odes, whereunto I must plainly confess to have seen yet nothing parallel in our language: *Ipsa mollities.*'

Whatever the experimental variety of texture, the masque as a whole is unified by the young poet's passionate purity of vision, which casts its spell with the opening,

> Before the starry threshold of Jove's court
> My mansion is,

and culminates in the incantation,

> Or if virtue feeble were,
> Heav'n itself would stoop to her.

(On the masque, see also below, pp. 346 ff.)

1–17 Cf. Plato, *Phaedo* 109–10. Here, as in *Comus* generally, classical and Christian images and ideas are blended.

2 mansion John 14.2

4 Cf. *Odyssey* 6.43–44. The Cambridge Manuscript contains, after line 4, a passage of 14 lines which Milton deleted. The main part of the passage was this:

> Amidst th' Hesperian gardens, on whose banks
> Bedewed with nectar and celestial songs
> Eternal roses grow, and hyacinth
> And fruits of golden rind, on whose fair tree
> The scaly-harnessed dragon ever keeps
> His unenchanted eye; and round the verge
> And sacred limits of this blissful isle
> The jealous ocean, that old river, winds
> His far-extended arms, till with steep fall
> Half his waste flood the wide Atlantic fills
> And half the slow, unfadomed Stygian pool. . . .

5 smoke and stir Cf. *Od.* 3.29.12, *fumium et opes strepitumque Romae*

7 pinfold pen for animals

9 crown 1 Cor. 9.25; Rev. 2.10

10 mortal change death

11 Rev. 4.4

12–14 Cf. *Aen.* 6.129–31

13 key cf. *Lycidas* 111

The Mask

The Persons
The Attendant Spirit afterwards in the habit of Thyrsis
Comus with his crew
The Lady
1st Brother
2nd Brother
Sabrina the Nymph

The first scene discovers a wild wood. The Attendant Spirit descends or enters.

Before the starry threshold of Jove's court
My mansion is, where those immortal shapes
Of bright aerial spirits live enspher'd
In regions mild of calm and serene air,
Above the smoke and stir of this dim spot,   5
Which men call earth, and with low-thoughted care
Confin'd and pester'd in this pinfold here,
Strive to keep up a frail and feverish being
Unmindful of the crown that virtue gives
After this mortal change to her true servants   10
Amongst the enthron'd gods on sainted seats.
Yet some there be that by due steps aspire
To lay their just hands on that golden key
That opes the palace of eternity:
To such my errand is, and but for such,   15
I would not soil these pure ambrosial weeds

17 mould the earth? the flesh?

20 Jove (Jupiter, Zeus) ruled the heavens, Pluto (**'nether Jove'**) the under-world, and **Neptune** (Poseidon) the sea.

30 tract Wales and the Welsh-English border
31 peer the Earl of Bridgewater   **mickle** great

33 proud in arms cf. *Aen.* 1.21

37 Cf. *Aen.* 9.391–92
37–9 A wood is a traditional symbol for life and its hazards; cf. Dante, *Inf.* 1; Spenser, *F.Q.* 1.1.7 f.

With the rank vapours of this sin-worn mould.
  But to my task. Neptune besides the sway
Of every salt flood and each ebbing stream
Took in by lot 'twixt high, and nether Jove   20
Imperial rule of all the sea-girt isles
That like to rich and various gems inlay
The unadorned bosom of the deep,
Which he to grace his tributary gods
By course commits to several government   25
And gives them leave to wear their sapphire crowns
And wield their little tridents, but this isle
The greatest and the best of all the main
He quarters to his blue-hair'd deities,
And all this tract that fronts the falling sun   30
A noble peer of mickle trust and power
Has in his charge, with temper'd awe to guide
An old and haughty nation proud in arms:
Where his fair offspring nurs'd in princely lore
Are coming to attend their father's state   35
And new-entrusted sceptre, but their way
Lies through the perplex'd paths of this drear wood,
The nodding horror of whose shady brows
Threats the forlorn and wand'ring passenger.
And here their tender age might suffer peril,   40
But that by quick command from sov'reign Jove
I was despatch'd for their defence, and guard;
And listen why, for I will tell you now
What never yet was heard in tale or song
From old or modern bard in hall, or bow'r.   45
  Bacchus, that first from out the purple grape
Crush'd the sweet poison of misused wine

48 Bacchus, carried off by pirates, changed them into dolphins (Ovid, *Met.* 3.605–86). Milton's phrase is a Latinism for 'after the transformation of'.

58 The Greek name Comus means 'revelry' or 'band of revellers'; he had been personified by Renaissance writers (starting from the *Imagines* of the ancient Philostratus).

66 drought of Phoebus thirst caused by the sun's heat

69 Gen. 1.27

72–7 Circe's victims, while completely transformed, remembered that they had been human. Milton, in having the face only changed, may have followed such a precedent as Ariosto (*Orlando Furioso* 6.60–66) for convenience of stage presentation.

After the Tuscan mariners transform'd
Coasting the Tyrrhene shore, as the winds listed
On Circe's island fell (who knows not Circe   50
The daughter of the Sun? Whose charmed cup
Whoever tasted lost his upright shape
And downward fell into a grovelling swine)
This nymph that gaz'd upon his clust'ring locks
With ivy berries wreath'd, and his blithe youth   55
Had by him ere he parted thence, a son
Much like his father, but his mother more,
Whom therefore she brought up, and Comus nam'd,
Who ripe and frolic of his full-grown age,
Roving the Celtic, and Iberian fields,   60
At last betakes him to this ominous wood,
And in thick shelter of black shade embower'd,
Excels his mother at her mighty art,
Off'ring to every weary traveller
His orient liquor in a crystal glass   65
To quench the drought of Phoebus, which as they taste
(For most do taste through fond intemperate thirst)
Soon as the potion works, their human count'nance,
Th' express resemblance of the gods, is chang'd
Into some brutish form of wolf or bear   70
Or ounce, or tiger, hog, or bearded goat,
All other parts remaining as they were,
And they, so perfect is their misery,
Not once perceive their foul disfigurement,
But boast themselves more comely than before   75
And all their friends and native home forget
To roll with pleasure in a sensual sty.
Therefore when any favour'd of high Jove

80   **glancing** shooting, gleaming

93   **star** Hesperus (Venus)   **fold** put sheep in the fold

96   **allay** temper, cool

98   **upward** The sun is now below the horizon.

100–1   Ps. 19.4–5

Chances to pass through this advent'rous glade,
Swift as the sparkle of a glancing star   80
I shoot from heav'n to give him safe convoy
As now I do: but first I must put off
These my sky-robes spun out of Iris' woof
And take the weeds and likeness of a swain
That to the service of this house belongs,   85
Who with his soft pipe and smooth-dittied song
Well knows to still the wild winds when they roar,
And hush the waving woods, nor of less faith,
And in the office of his mountain watch,
Likeliest and nearest to the present aid   90
Of this occasion. But I hear the tread
Of hateful steps, I must be viewless now.

*Comus enters with a charming rod in one hand, his glass
in the other, with him a rout of monsters headed like sundry
sorts of wild beasts, but otherwise like men and women,
their apparel glistering; they come in making a riotous and
unruly noise, with torches in their hands.*

Comus
The star that bids the shepherd fold,
Now the top of heav'n doth hold,
And the gilded car of day   95
His glowing axle doth allay
In the steep Atlantic stream,
And the slope sun his upward beam
Shoots against the dusky pole,
Pacing toward the other goal   100
Of his chamber in the east.

105 rosy twine intertwined roses

113 watchful spheres See Plato, *Timaeus* 40; and *Vacation Exercise* 40 and note.

115 finny drove in Spenser, *F.Q.* 3.8.29.9

116 morris morris dance

118 pert lively **dapper** small and nimble

129 Cotytto a Thracian divinity celebrated in licentious nocturnal rites

Meanwhile welcome joy and feast,
Midnight shout, and revelry,
Tipsy dance, and jollity.
Braid your locks with rosy twine   105
Dropping odours, dropping wine.
Rigour now is gone to bed,
And advice with scrupulous head,
Strict age, and sour severity
With their grave saws in slumber lie.   110
We that are of purer fire
Imitate the starry choir,
Who in their nightly watchful spheres
Lead in swift round the months and years.
The sounds and seas with all their finny drove   115
Now to the moon in wavering morris move,
And on the tawny sands and shelves
Trip the pert fairies, and the dapper elves.
By dimpled brook and fountain brim,
The wood-nymphs deck'd with daisies trim   120
Their merry wakes and pastimes keep:
What hath night to do with sleep?
Night has better sweets to prove,
Venus now wakes, and wak'ns Love.
Come let us our rites begin,   125
'Tis only daylight that makes sin
Which these dun shades will ne'er report.
Hail goddess of nocturnal sport,
Dark-veil'd Cotytto, t' whom the secret flame
Of midnight torches burns; mysterious dame   130
That ne'er art call'd, but when the dragon womb
Of Stygian darkness spits her thickest gloom

139 morn Aurora **Indian steep** cf. *A Midsummer Night's Dream* 2.1.69

141 descry reveal

154 spongy absorbing
155 blear deceptive
156 presentments pictures

And makes one blot of all the air,
Stay thy cloudy ebon chair,
Wherein thou rid'st with Hecat', and befriend   135
Us thy vow'd priests till utmost end
Of all thy dues be done and none left out,
Ere the blabbing eastern scout,
The nice morn on th' Indian steep
From her cabin'd loophole peep,   140
And to the tell-tale sun descry
Our conceal'd solemnity.
Come, knit hands, and beat the ground,
In a light fantastic round.

The Measure

Break off, break off, I feel the different pace   145
Of some chaste footing near about this ground,
Run to your shrouds within these brakes and trees,
Our number may affright. Some virgin sure
(For so I can distinguish by mine art)
Benighted in these woods. Now to my charms,   150
And to my wily trains; I shall ere long
Be well stock'd with as fair a herd as graz'd
About my mother Circe. Thus I hurl
My dazzling spells into the spongy air,
Of power to cheat the eye with blear illusion   155
And give it false presentments, lest the place
And my quaint habits breed astonishment
And put the damsel to suspicious flight,
Which must not be, for that's against my course;
I under fair pretence of friendly ends   160
And well-plac'd words of glozing courtesy

167 This line did not appear in the 1673 edition and is omitted in the *Works* so that, from here on, the Columbia line-numbering differs from that of most other editions.

168 fairly quietly

169 This, the reading of the Manuscript and of 1637 and 1645, was changed in the 1673 Errata to 'And hearken, if I may her business hear'—perhaps by a printer who did not understand Milton's use of 'hearken' as a transitive verb.

175 granges barns

189 a . . . weeds a sober person under a religious vow, in the garb of a pilgrim to the Holy Land

Baited with reasons not unplausible
Wind me into the easy-hearted man,
And hug him into snares. When once her eye
Hath met the virtue of this magic dust,   165
I shall appear some harmless villager
Whom thrift keeps up about his country gear.
But here she comes, I fairly step aside
And hearken, if I may, her business here.

The Lady enters

Lady
This way the noise was, if mine ear be true,   170
My best guide now; methought it was the sound
Of riot and ill-manag'd merriment,
Such as the jocund flute or gamesome pipe
Stirs up amongst the loose unletter'd hinds,
When for their teeming flocks, and granges full   175
In wanton dance they praise the bounteous Pan
And thank the gods amiss. I should be loth
To meet the rudeness and swill'd insolence
Of such late wassailers; yet O where else
Shall I inform my unacquainted feet   180
In the blind maze of this tangl'd wood?
My brothers when they saw me wearied out
With this long way, resolving here to lodge
Under the spreading favour of these pines,
Stepp'd, as they said, to the next thicket side   185
To bring me berries, or such cooling fruit
As the kind hospitable woods provide.
They left me then, when the grey-hooded ev'n
Like a sad votarist in palmer's weeds

195–225   These lines were not in the acting version; they appeared in the editions of 1637 and 1645.

204   single only, total

212   siding defending

214   flittering (MS.) hovering

Rose from the hindmost wheels of Phoebus' wain.   190
But where they are and why they came not back
Is now the labour of my thoughts; 'tis likeliest
They had engag'd their wand'ring steps too far,
And envious darkness, ere they could return,
Had stol'n them from me; else O thievish night   195
Why shouldst thou, but for some felonious end,
In thy dark lantern thus close up the stars
That nature hung in heav'n, and fill'd their lamps
With everlasting oil, to give due light
To the misled and lonely traveller?   200
This is the place, as well as I may guess,
Whence ev'n now the tumult of loud mirth
Was rife and perfect in my list'ning ear,
Yet nought but single darkness do I find.
What might this be? A thousand fantasies   205
Begin to throng into my memory
Of calling shapes, and beck'ning shadows dire,
And airy tongues, that syllable men's names
On sands, and shores, and desert wildernesses.
These thoughts may startle well, but not astound   210
The virtuous mind, that ever walks attended
By a strong siding champion conscience—
O welcome pure-ey'd faith, white-handed hope,
Thou flittering angel girt with golden wings,
And thou unblemish'd form of chastity,   215
I see ye visibly, and now believe
That he, the supreme good, t' whom all things ill
Are but as slavish officers of vengeance,
Would send a glist'ring guardian if need were
To keep my life and honour unassail'd.   220

221–4 The repeated lines suggest a symbolic confirmation of the inward assurance of lines 216–20.

231 **airy cell** (MS, shell) an actua lcavern or vault of air

232 **Maeander** a winding river in Asia Minor

241   Cf. *At a Solemn Music* 2

Was I deceiv'd, or did a sable cloud
Turn forth her silver lining on the night?
I did not err, there does a sable cloud
Turn forth her silver lining on the night
And casts a gleam over this tufted grove.   225
I cannot hallo to my brothers, but
Such noise as I can make to be heard farthest
I'll venture, for my new-enliv'n'd spirits
Prompt me; and they perhaps are not far off.

Song

Sweet Echo, sweetest nymph that liv'st unseen   230
     Within thy airy cell
  By slow Maeander's margent green,
And in the violet-embroider'd vale
  Where the love-lorn nightingale
Nightly to thee her sad song mourneth well.   235
Canst thou not tell me of a gentle pair
  That likest thy Narcissus are?
    O if thou have
  Hid them in some flowry cave,
    Tell me but where   240
Sweet queen of parley, daughter of the sphere,
 So mayst thou be translated to the skies,
And give resounding grace to all heav'n's harmonies.

Comus
Can any mortal mixture of earth's mould
Breathe such divine enchanting ravishment?   245
Sure something holy lodges in that breast,

251 fall cadence

253 The sirens whose singing put a spell upon sailors (*Odyssey* 12.47 f., 165 f.).

And with these raptures moves the vocal air
To testify his hidd'n residence;
How sweetly did they float upon the wings
Of silence, through the empty-vaulted night,   250
At every fall smoothing the raven down
Of darkness till she smil'd: I have oft heard
My mother Circe with the Sirens three,
Amidst the flowery-kirtl'd Naiades
Culling their potent herbs, and baleful drugs,   255
Who as they sung, would take the prison'd soul,
And lap it in Elysium; Scylla wept,
And chid her barking waves into attention,
And fell Charybdis murmur'd soft applause:
Yet they in pleasing slumber lull'd the sense,   260
And in sweet madness rob'd it of itself,
But such a sacred, and home-felt delight,
Such sober certainty of waking bliss
I never heard till now. I'll speak to her
And she shall be my queen. Hail foreign wonder   265
Whom certain these rough shades did never breed
Unless the goddess that in rural shrine
Dwell'st here with Pan or Sylvan, by blest song
Forbidding every bleak unkindly fog
To touch the prosperous growth of this tall wood.   270
Lady
Nay gentle shepherd, ill is lost that praise
That is address'd to unattending ears,
Not any boast of skill, but extreme shift
How to regain my sever'd company
Compell'd me to awake the courteous Echo   275
To give me answer from her mossy couch.

277–90   Dialogue in single lines, the stichomythia of Greek drama

Comus
What chance good lady, hath bereft you thus?
Lady
Dim darkness, and this leafy labyrinth.
Comus
Could that divide you from near-ushering guides?
Lady
They left me weary on a grassy turf.   280
Comus
By falsehood, or discourtesy, or why?
Lady
To seek i' the valley some cool friendly spring.
Comus
And left your fair side all unguarded lady?
Lady
They were but twain, and purpos'd quick return.
Comus
Perhaps forestalling night prevented them.   285
Lady
How easy my misfortune is to hit!
Comus
Imports their loss, beside the present need?
Lady
No less than if I should my brothers loose.
Comus
Were they of manly prime, or youthful bloom?
Lady
As smooth as Hebe's their unrazor'd lips.   290
Comus
Two such I saw, what time the labour'd ox
In his loose traces from the furrow came,

293 swink'd hedger weary hedge-clipper, labourer

301 plighted folded

313 bosky bourn brook bordered with bushes

318 thatch'd pallet straw nest

And the swink'd hedger at his supper sat;
I saw 'em under a green mantling vine
That crawls along the side of yon small hill,   295
Plucking ripe clusters from the tender shoots,
Their port was more than human, as they stood;
I took it for a faery vision
Of some gay creatures of the element
That in the colours of the rainbow live   300
And play i' the plighted clouds. I was awe-struck,
And as I pass'd, I worshipp'd; if those you seek
It were a journey like the path to heav'n,
To help you find them.
Lady   Gentle villager
What readiest way would bring me to that place?   305
Comus
Due west it rises from this shrubby point.
Lady
To find out that, good shepherd, I suppose,
In such a scant allowance of star-light,
Would overtask the best land-pilot's art,
Without the sure guess of well-practis'd feet.   310
Comus
I know each lane, and every alley green
Dingle, or bushy dell of this wide wood,
And every bosky bourn from side to side
My daily walks and ancient neighbourhood,
And if your stray attendance be yet lodg'd,   315
Or shroud within these limits, I shall know
Ere morrow wake, or the low-roosted lark
From her thatch'd pallet rouse, if otherwise
I can conduct you lady, to a low

323-5 A traditional and especially pastoral sentiment; cf. Aeschylus, *Agamemnon* 772 f.; Horace, *Od.* 3.29.14–16; etc.

326   yet still

334   disinherit dispossess

341   star of Arcady constellation of the Great Bear, by which Greek mariners steered. Callisto, daughter of the Arcadian king Lycaon, was loved by Zeus, changed into the Great Bear; her son Areas became the Lesser or Little Bear (342).
342   Tyrian Cynosure the North or Pole Star in the Little Bear, by which Phoenician sailors navigated
344   wattled cotes sheepfolds made of plaited branches

But loyal cottage, where you may be safe   320
Till further quest.
Lady   Shepherd I take thy word,
And trust thy honest offer'd courtesy,
Which oft is sooner found in lowly sheds
With smoky rafters, than in tap'stry halls
And courts of princes, where it first was nam'd,   325
And yet is most pretended: in a place
Less warranted than this, or less secure
I cannot be, that I should fear to change it;
Eye me blest providence, and square my trial
To my proportion'd strength. Shepherd lead on.   330

The two Brothers

Elder Brother
Unmuffle ye faint stars, and thou fair moon
That wont'st to love the traveller's benison,
Stoop thy pale visage through an amber cloud,
And disinherit Chaos, that reigns here
In double night of darkness, and of shades;   335
Or if your influence be quite damm'd up
With black usurping mists, some gentle taper
Though a rush-candle from the wicker hole
Of some clay habitation visit us
With thy long levell'd rule of streaming light,   340
And thou shalt be our star of Arcady,
Or Tyrian Cynosure.
2nd Brother   Or if our eyes
Be barr'd that happiness, might we but hear
The folded flocks penn'd in their wattled cotes,
Or sound of pastoral reed with oaten stops,   345

373–4 Cf.Spenser, *F.Q.* 1.1.12.9

Or whistle from the lodge, or village cock
Count the night watches to his feathery dames,
'Twould be some solace yet, some little cheering
In this close dungeon of innumerous boughs.
But O that hapless virgin our lost sister,   350
Where may she wander now, whither betake her
From the chill dew, amongst rude burs and thistles?
Perhaps some cold bank is her bolster now
Or 'gainst the rugged bark of some broad elm
Leans her unpillow'd head fraught with sad fears.   355
What if in wild amazement, and affright,
Or while we speak within the direful grasp
Of savage hunger, or of savage heat?
Elder Brother
Peace brother, be not over-exquisite
To cast the fashion of uncertain evils;   360
For grant they be so, while they rest unknown,
What need a man forestall his date of grief,
And run to meet what he would most avoid?
Or if they be but false alarms of fear,
How bitter is such self-delusion?   365
I do not think my sister so to seek,
Or so unprincipl'd in virtue's book,
And the sweet peace that goodness bosoms ever,
As that the single want of light and noise
(Not being in danger, as I trust she is not)   370
Could stir the constant mood of her calm thoughts,
And put them into misbecoming plight.
Virtue could see to do what Virtue would
By her own radiant light, though sun and moon
Were in the flat sea sunk. And Wisdom's self   375

377–8   For the image of wings see Plato, *Phaedrus* 246 f.

380   **to-ruffl'd**   much ruffled ('to' is an archaic intensive prefix)

382   **centre**   i.e., of the earth

395   **unenchanted**   that cannot be enchanted; cf. the cancelled lines quoted in the note on 4 above

401   **Danger**   power   **wink on**   close the eyes to

404   **it recks me not**   I am not concerned about

Oft seeks to sweet retired solitude,
Where with her best nurse Contemplation
She plumes her feathers, and lets grow her wings
That in the various bustle of resort
Were all to-ruffl'd, and sometimes impair'd.   380
He that has light within his own clear breast
May sit i' the centre, and enjoy bright day,
But he that hides a dark soul, and foul thoughts
Benighted walks under the midday sun;
Himself is his own dungeon.   385
2nd Brother   'Tis most true
That musing Meditation most affects
The pensive secrecy of desert cell,
Far from the cheerful haunt of men, and herds,
And sits as safe as in a senate-house,
For who would rob a hermit of his weeds,   390
His few books, or his beads, or maple dish,
Or do his grey hairs any violence?
But Beauty like the fair Hesperian tree
Laden with blooming gold, had need the guard
Of dragon-watch with unenchanted eye,   395
To save her blossoms and defend her fruit
From the rash hand of bold Incontinence.
You may as well spread out the unsunn'd heaps
Of miser's treasure by an outlaw's den,
And tell me it is safe, as bid me hope   400
Danger will wink on opportunity,
And let a single helpless maiden pass
Uninjur'd in this wild surrounding waste.
Of night, or loneliness it recks me not,
I fear the dread events that dog them both,   405

407   unowned unprotected

422   quiver'd nymph nymph with a quiver of arrows, a follower of the huntress Diana, goddess of chastity
423   unharbour'd without shelter

430   unblench'd fearless

433   fire of. *L'Allegro* 104

Lest some ill greeting touch attempt the person
Of our unowned sister.
Elder Brother   I do not, brother,
Infer, as if I thought my sister's state
Secure without all doubt, or controversy:
Yet where an equal poise of hope and fear   410
Does arbitrate th' event, my nature is
That I incline to hope, rather than fear,
And banish gladly squint suspicion.
My sister is not so defenceless left
As you imagine, she has a hidden strength   415
Which you remember not.
2nd Brother   What hidden strength,
Unless the strength of heav'n, if you mean that?
Elder Brother
I mean that too, but yet a hidden strength
Which if heav'n gave it, may be term'd her own:
'Tis chastity, my brother, chastity: 420
She that has that, is clad in complete steel,
And like a quiver'd nymph with arrows keen
May trace huge forests, and unharbour'd heaths,
Infamous hills, and sandy perilous wilds,
Where through the sacred rays of chastity,   425
No savage fierce, bandit, or mountaineer
Will dare to soil her virgin purity;
Yea there, where very desolation dwells
By grots, and caverns shagg'd with horrid shades,
She may pass on with unblench'd majesty,   430
Be it not done in pride, or in presumption.
Some say no evil thing that walks by night
In fog, or fire, by lake, or moory fen,

434 hag evil spirit in female form **unlaid** unexorcised, wandering from his proper abode
435 Spirits might walk between curfew time (eight or nine o'clock) and the first crowing of the cock. Cf. *Nativity* 229–36.
436 faery . . . mine underground spirit

439 schools philosophical schools, teachings

448 Minerva Pallas Athene, the virgin goddess of wisdom and war, who sprang full-grown from the head of Zeus and whose shield bore the head of the Gorgon Medusa

458 Cf. *Arcades* 72–73

463–75 A free paraphrase of Plato, *Phaedo* 81

Blue meagre hag, or stubborn unlaid ghost,
That breaks his magic chains at curfew time,   435
No goblin, or swart faery of the mine,
Has hurtful power o'er true virginity.
Do ye believe me yet, or shall I call
Antiquity from the old schools of Greece
To testify the arms of chastity?   440
Hence had the huntress Dian her dread bow,
Fair silver-shafted queen for ever chaste,
Wherewith she tam'd the brinded lioness
And spotted mountain pard, but set at nought
The frivolous bolt of Cupid; gods and men   445
Fear'd her stern frown, and she was queen o' the woods.
What was the snaky-headed Gorgon shield
That wise Minerva wore, unconquer'd virgin,
Wherewith she freez'd her foes to congeal'd stone?
But rigid looks of chaste austerity,   450
And noble grace that dash'd brute violence
With sudden adoration, and blank awe.
So dear to heav'n is saintly chastity,
That when a soul is found sincerely so,
A thousand liveried angels lackey her,   455
Driving far off each thing of sin and guilt,
And in clear dream, and solemn vision
Tell her of things that no gross ear can hear,
Till oft converse with heav'nly habitants
Begin to cast a beam on th' outward shape,   460
The unpolluted temple of the mind,
And turns it by degrees to the soul's essence,
Till all be made immortal: but when lust
By unchaste looks, loose gestures, and foul talk,

474   sensual'ty (1637, 1673) sensualty (1645)

478   Cf. *Love's Labour's Lost* 4.3.342–3

483   night-founder'd benighted

But most by lewd and lavish act of sin,   465
Lets in defilement to the inward parts,
The soul grows clotted by contagion,
Embodies, and imbrutes, till she quite lose
The divine property of her first being.
Such are those thick and gloomy shadows damp   470
Oft seen in charnel-vaults, and sepulchres
Hovering, and sitting by a new-made grave,
As loth to leave the body that it lov'd,
And link'd itself by carnal sensual'ty
To a degenerate and degraded state.   475
2nd Brother
How charming is divine philosophy!
Not harsh, and crabbed as dull fools suppose,
But musical as is Apollo's lute,
And a perpetual feast of nectar'd sweets,
Where no crude surfeit reigns.   480
Elder Brother   List, list, I hear
Some far-off hallo break the silent air.
2nd Brother
Methought so too; what should it be?
Elder Brother   For certain
Either some one like us night-founder'd here,
Or else some neighbour woodman, or at worst,
Some roving robber calling to his fellows.   485
2nd Brother
Heav'n keep my sister! Again, again and near,
Best draw, and stand upon our guard.
Elder Brother   I'll hallo,
If he be friendly he comes well, if not,
Defence is a good cause, and heav'n be for us.

491   iron stakes their swords

495   huddling piling up, crowding
495–512   A passage of rhymed couplets

506   To compared with

The Attendant Spirit habited like a shepherd

That hallo I should know, what are you? speak;   490
Come not too near, you fall on iron stakes else.
Spirit
What voice is that, my young lord? speak again.
2nd Brother
O brother, 'tis my father's shepherd sure.
Elder Brother
Thyrsis? Whose artful strains have oft delayed
The huddling brook to hear his madrigal,   495
And sweeten'd every musk-rose of the dale,
How cam'st thou here good swain? hath any ram
Slipp'd from his fold, or young kid lost his dam,
Or straggling wether the pent flock forsook?
How couldst thou find this dark sequester'd nook?   500
Spirit
O my lov'd master's heir, and his next joy,
I came not here on such a trivial toy
As a stray'd ewe, or to pursue the stealth
Of pilfering wolf, not all the fleecy wealth
That doth enrich these downs, is worth a thought   505
To this my errand, and the care it brought.
But O my virgin lady, where is she?
How chance she is not in your company?
Elder Brother
To tell thee sadly shepherd, without blame,
Or our neglect, we lost her as we came.   510
Spirit
Ay me unhappy! then my fears are true.
Elder Brother
What fears good Thyrsis? Prithee briefly shew.

513-19 The allegorical interpretation of pagan myth began before Plato and continued throughout the Christian era (and was early extended to the Bible); cf. *Comus* itself and the quotations from Sandys in the headnote. One motive was the common belief that pagan myth was not merely fiction but a partly distorted version of Hebraic and Christian truth; cf. *P.L.* 10.5 81-84 and note.

520   navel centre

530   Character'd engraved
531   crofts small enclosed fields
532   brow overlook

540   then the time that

Spirit
I'll tell you. 'Tis not vain, or fabulous,
(Though so esteem'd by shallow ignorance)
What the sage poets taught by th' heav'nly Muse,   515
Storied of old in high immortal verse
Of dire chimeras and enchanted isles,
And rifted rocks whose entrance leads to hell,
For such there be, but unbelief is blind.
   Within the navel of this hideous wood,   520
Immur'd in cypress shades a sorcerer dwells
Of Bacchus and of Circe born, great Comus,
Deep skill'd in all his mother's witcheries,
And here to every thirsty wanderer
By sly enticement gives his baneful cup,   525
With many murmurs mix'd, whose pleasing poison
The visage quite transforms of him that drinks,
And the inglorious likeness of a beast
Fixes instead, unmoulding reason's mintage
Character'd in the face; this have I learnt   530
Tending my flocks hard by i' the hilly crofts
That brow this bottom glade, whence night by night
He and his monstrous rout are heard to howl
Like stabl'd wolves, or tigers at their prey,
Doing abhorred rites to Hecate   535
In their obscured haunts of inmost bowers.
Yet have they many baits, and guileful spells
T' inveigle and invite th' unwary sense
Of them that pass unweeting by the way.
This evening late by then the chewing flocks   540
Had ta'en their supper on the savoury herb
Of knot-grass dew-besprent, and were in fold,

547   meditate . . . minstrelsy play on shepherd's pipe (cf. Virgil, *Ecl.* 1.2

553   drowsy frighted frightened though drowsy. This is the reading of the editions of 1637, 1645, and 1673; some editors prefer the 'drowsy flighted' of the MS.

556   steam (1637, 1645) 1673, stream

559–60   be . . . displac'd no longer exist, if she could always be destroyed by such music

I sat me down to watch upon a bank
With ivy canopied, and interwove
With flaunting honeysuckle, and began   545
Wrapt in a pleasing fit of melancholy
To meditate my rural minstrelsy,
Till fancy had her fill, but ere a close
The wonted roar was up amidst the woods,
And fill'd the air with barbarous dissonance,   550
At which I ceas'd, and listen'd them a while,
Till an unusual stop of sudden silence
Gave respite to the drowsy frighted steeds
That draw the litter of close-curtain'd sleep.
At last a soft and solemn breathing sound   555
Rose like a steam of rich distill'd perfumes
And stole upon the air, that even silence
Was took ere she was ware, and wish'd she might
Deny her nature, and be never more
Still to be so displac'd. I was all ear,   560
And took in strains that might create a soul
Under the ribs of death, but O ere long
Too well I did perceive it was the voice
Of my most honour'd lady, your dear sister.
Amaz'd I stood, harrow'd with grief and fear,   565
And O poor hapless nightingale thought I,
How sweet thou sing'st, how near the deadly snare!
Then down the lawns I ran with headlong haste
Through paths and turnings oft'n trod by day,
Till guided by mine ear I found the place   570
Where that damn'd wizard hid in sly disguise
(For so by certain signs I knew) had met
Already, ere my best speed could prevent,

585 **period** sentence
586 **for me** by me, for my part

598 **firmament** sphere of fixed stars

The aidless innocent lady his wish'd prey,
Who gently ask'd if he had seen such two, 575
Supposing him some neighbour villager;
Longer I durst not stay, but soon I guess'd
Ye were the two she meant; with that I sprung
Into swift flight, till I had found you here,
But further know I not. 580
2nd Brother   O night and shades,
How are ye join'd with hell in triple knot
Against th' unarmed weakness of one virgin
Alone, and helpless! Is this the confidence
You gave me brother?
Elder Brother Yes, and keep it still,
Lean on it safely, not a period 585
Shall be unsaid for me: against the threats
Of malice or of sorcery, or that power
Which erring men call chance, this I hold firm,
Virtue may be assail'd, but never hurt,
Surpris'd by unjust force, but not enthrall'd, 590
Yea even that which mischief meant most harm
Shall in the happy trial prove most glory.
But evil on itself shall back recoil,
And mix no more with goodness, when at last
Gather'd like scum, and settl'd to itself 595
It shall be in eternal restless change
Self-fed, and self-consum'd; if this fail,
The pillar'd firmament is rott'nness,
And earth's base built on stubble. But come let's on.
Against th' opposing will and arm of heav'n 600
May never this just sword be lifted up,
But for that damn'd magician, let him be girt

605   Cf. *P.L.* 2.628 **bugs** (MS), forms

607   **purchase** prey

608–9   **and . . . hips** (MS) other editions, 'to a foul death,/Curs'd as his life'

619 f.   The account of the 'shepherd lad' with his 'simples' (medicinal herbs) may be only a dramatic invention or may include a half-playful tribute to Milton's friend Diodati, the medical student (cf. *Epitaphium Damonis* 150–2).

620   **small . . . to** unimpressive appearance

With all the grisly legions that troop
Under the sooty flag of Acheron,
Harpies and hydras, or all the monstrous bugs   605
'Twixt Africa and Ind. I'll find him out,
And force him to restore his purchase back,
Or drag him by the curls and cleave his scalp
Down to the hips.
Spirit   Alas good vent'rous youth,
I love thy courage yet, and bold emprise,   610
But here thy sword can do thee little stead;
Far other arms and other weapons must
Be those that quell the might of hellish charms,
He with his bare wand can unthread thy joints,
And crumble all thy sinews.
Elder Brother   Why prithee shepherd,   615
How durst thou then thyself approach so near
As to make this relation?
Spirit   Care and utmost shifts
How to secure the Lady from surprisal
Brought to my mind a certain shepherd lad
Of small regard to see to, yet well skill'd   620
In every virtuous plant and healing herb
That spreads her verdant leaf to th' morning ray;
He lov'd me well, and oft would beg me sing,
Which when I did, he on the tender grass
Would sit and hearken ev'n to ecstasy,   625
And in requital ope his leathern scrip,
And show me simples of a thousand names
Telling their strange and vigorous faculties;
Amongst the rest a small unsightly root,
But of divine effect, he cull'd me out;   630

632   another country heaven? Cf. the quotations from Sandys in the head-note.

635   clouted shoon hobnailed and/or patched shoes

636   moly the magical plant, given by Hermes to Odysseus, which protected him from Circe's spells (*Odyssey* 10.287 f.)

638   haemony The plant apparently represents Platonic-Christian temper-ance (see the headnote above); if it were religious faith or divine grace, its efficacy would surely be less limited than it proves to be.

646   lime-twigs Birds were once caught by lime smeared on branches.

651–2   Cf. Spenser, *F.Q.* 2.12.57

655   Cf. *Aen.* 8.193–261

The leaf was darkish, and had prickles on it,
But in another country, as he said,
Bore a bright golden flow'r, but not in this soil:
Unknown, and like esteem'd, and the dull swain
Treads on it daily with his clouted shoon,   635
And yet more med'cinal is it than that moly
Which Hermes once to wise Ulysses gave;
He call'd it haemony, and gave it me,
And bade me keep it as of sov'reign use
'Gainst all enchantments, mildew blast, or damp   640
Or ghastly Furies' apparition;
I purs'd it up, but little reck'ning made,
Till now that this extremity compell'd,
But now I find it true; for by this means
I knew the foul enchanter though disguis'd   645
Enter'd the very lime-twigs of his spells,
And yet came off: if you have this about you
(As I will give you when we go) you may
Boldly assault the necromancer's hall;
Where if he be, with dauntless hardihood,   650
And brandish'd blade rush on him, break his glass,
And shed the luscious liquor on the ground
But seize his wand; though he and his curs'd crew
Fierce sign of battle make, and menace high,
Or like the sons of Vulcan vomit smoke,   655
Yet will they soon retire, if he but shrink.
Elder Brother
Thyrsis lead on apace, I'll follow thee,
And some good angel bear a shield before us.

The scene changes to a stately palace, set out with all manner of deliciousness: soft music, tables spread with all dainties.

675–6 See the *Odyssey* 4.219–30
675 **Nepenthes** magic potion, opiate
676 **Helena** Helen of Troy, daughter of Zeus

*Comus appears with his rabble, and the Lady set in an
enchanted chair, to whom he offers his glass; which she
puts by, and goes about to rise.*

Comus
Nay lady sit; if I but wave this wand,
Your nerves are all chain'd up in alabaster   660
And you a statue; or as Daphne was
Root-bound, that fled Apollo.
Lady   Fool do not boast,
Thou canst not touch the freedom of my mind
With all thy charms, although this corporal rind
Thou hast immanacl'd, while heav'n sees good.   665
Comus
Why are you vex'd lady? why do you frown?
Here dwell no frowns, nor anger, from these gates
Sorrow flies far: see here be all the pleasures
That fancy can beget on youthful thoughts,
When the fresh blood grows lively, and returns   670
Brisk as the April buds in primrose season.
And first behold this cordial julep here
That flames, and dances in his crystal bounds
With spirits of balm, and fragrant syrups mix'd.
Not that Nepenthes which the wife of Thone   675
In Egypt gave to Jove-born Helena
Is of such power to stir up joy as this,
To life so friendly, or so cool to thirst.
Why should you be so cruel to yourself,
And to those dainty limbs which nature lent   680
For gentle usage, and soft delicacy?
But you invert the cov'nants of her trust,
And harshly deal like an ill borrower

685 unexempt universal

700 lickerish tempting

707 budge stiff, formal (from a kind of fur used on doctoral hoods or robes)

708 Cynic tub Diogenes, the Cynic philosopher of Athens, was said to have lived in a tub to show his scorn for luxury.

With that which you receiv'd on other terms,
Scorning the unexempt condition   685
By which all mortal frailty must subsist,
Refreshment after toil, ease after pain,
That have been tir'd all day without repast,
And timely rest have wanted, but fair virgin,
This will restore all soon.
Lady   'Twill not false traitor,   690
'Twill not restore the truth and honesty
That thou hast banish'd from thy tongue with lies;
Was this the cottage, and the safe abode
Thou told'st me of? What grim aspects are these,
These ugly-headed monsters? Mercy guard me!   695
Hence with thy brew'd enchantments, foul deceiver;
Hast thou betray'd my credulous innocence
With vizor'd falsehood and base forgeries
And wouldst thou seek again to trap me here
With lickerish baits fit to ensnare a brute?   700
Were it a draught for Juno when she banquets,
I would not taste thy treasonous offer; none
But such as are good men can give good things,
And that which is not good is not delicious
To a well-govern'd and wise appetite.   705
Comus
O foolishness of men! that lend their ears
To those budge doctors of the Stoic fur,
And fetch their precepts from the Cynic tub,
Praising the lean and sallow abstinence.
Wherefore did nature pour her bounties forth   710
With such a full and unwithdrawing hand,
Covering the earth with odours, fruits, and flocks,

719 hutch'd laid away, hoarded

721 pet fit
722 frieze coarse woollen cloth

733 deep the earth, the vault of hell. Some minerals were thought to repro-
duce themselves.
734 they below inhabitants of the underworld

737 cozen'd cheated
737–55 Comus' specious arguments for the use of nature's bounties (706–36)
shift in 737–55 (lines which were not in the acting version) to a non-sequitur,
a plea for sexual licence in the common vein of Renaissance libertinism:
e.g., Marlowe, *Hero and Leander* 1.215 f., 315 f.; some of Donne's early poems;
Thomas Randolph, *Muses' Looking Glass* 2.3 ('Nature has been bountiful . . .').

Thronging the seas with spawn innumerable,
But all to please and sate the curious taste?
And set to work millions of spinning worms   715
That in their green shops weave the smooth-hair'd silk
To deck her sons, and that no corner might
Be vacant of her plenty, in her own loins
She hutch'd th' all-worshipp'd ore and precious gems
To store her children with; if all the world   720
Should in a pet of temperance feed on pulse,
Drink the clear stream, and nothing wear but frieze,
Th' all-giver would be unthank'd, would be unprais'd,
Not half his riches known, and yet despis'd,
And we should serve him as a grudging master,   725
As a penurious niggard of his wealth,
And live like nature's bastards, not her sons,
Who would be quite surcharg'd with her own weight
And strangl'd with her waste fertility;
Th' earth cumber'd, and the wing'd air dark'd with
        plumes,   730
The herds would over-multitude their lords,
The sea o'erfraught would swell, and th' unsought diamonds
Would so emblaze the forehead of the deep
And so bestud with stars that they below
Would grow inur'd to light, and come at last   735
To gaze upon the sun with shameless brows.
List lady be not coy, and be not cozen'd
With that same vaunted name virginity;
Beauty is nature's coin, must not be hoarded,
But must be current, and the good thereof   740
Consists in mutual and partak'n bliss,
Unsavoury in th' enjoyment of itself.

743–4   Cf. *A Midsummer Night's Dream* 1.1.76–78

751   **tease** comb, card
752   **vermeil** vermilion
753   **Love-darting eyes** cf. Sylvester, 2.3.4.849, 'love-darting eyn'

759   **prank'd** dressed up
760   **bolt** sift, refine

If you let slip time, like a neglected rose
It withers on the stalk with languish'd head.
Beauty is nature's brag, and must be shown   745
In courts, at feasts, on high solemnities
Where most may wonder at the workmanship;
It is for homely features to keep home,
They had their name thence; coarse complexions
And cheeks of sorry grain will serve to ply   750
The sampler, or to tease the housewife's wool.
What need a vermeil-tinctur'd lip for that,
Love-darting eyes, or tresses like the morn?
There was another meaning in these gifts,
Think what, and be advis'd, you are but young yet.   755
Lady
I had not thought to have unlocked my lips
In this unhallow'd air, but that this juggler
Would think to charm my judgement, as mine eyes
Obtruding false rules prank'd in reason's garb.
I hate when vice can bolt her arguments,   760
And virtue has no tongue to check her pride:
Imposter, do not charge most innocent nature,
As if she would her children should be riotous
With her abundance; she good cateress,
Means her provision only to the good   765
That live according to her sober laws
And holy dictate of spare temperance:
If every just man that now pines with want
Had but a moderate and beseeming share
Of that which lewdly-pamper'd luxury   770
Now heaps upon some few with vast excess,
Nature's full blessings would be well dispens'd

779–806   These lines were not in the acting version or the Cambridge Manuscript; they appeared in the editions of 1637 and 1645. In 762–99 the Lady replies, mainly in rational terms, to Comus' first argument and urges temperance and fair distribution of nature's blessings. In 779–99, replying to his second argument, she rises to an impassioned religious affirmation of the beauty of chastity.

785   **mystery** cf. *Apology for Smectymnuus* (quoted above, pp. 197 ff.)

791   **fence** art of fencing
792   **convinc'd** confuted

797   **brute earth** cf. Horace, *Od.* 1.34.9

In unsuperfluous ev'n proportion,
And she no whit encumber'd with her store,
And then the giver would be better thank'd,   775
His praise due paid, for swinish gluttony
Ne'er looks to heav'n amidst his gorgeous feast,
But with besotted base ingratitude
Crams, and blasphemes his feeder. Shall I go on?
Or have I said enough? To him that dares   780
Arm his profane tongue with contemptuous words
Against the sun-clad power of chastity,
Fain would I something say, yet to what end?
Thou hast nor ear, nor soul to apprehend
The sublime notion, and high mystery   785
That must be utter'd to unfold the sage
And serious doctrine of virginity,
And thou art worthy that thou shouldst not know
More happiness than this thy present lot.
Enjoy your dear wit, and gay rhetoric   790
That hath so well been taught her dazzling fence,
Thou art not fit to hear thyself convinc'd;
Yet should I try, the uncontrolled worth
Of this pure cause would kindle my rapt spirits
To such a flame of sacred vehemence,   795
That dumb things would be mov'd to sympathise,
And the brute earth would lend her nerves, and shake,
Till all thy magic structures rear'd so high,
Were shatter'd into heaps o'er thy false head.
Comus
She fables not, I feel that I do fear   800
Her words set off by some superior power;
And though not mortal, yet a cold shudd'ring dew

805   Saturn's crew the rebel Titans imprisoned in the underworld

808   canon laws . . . foundation. Cf. Comus' pose of priesthood in 93–144

810   One of the four humours of the body (blood, phlegm, choler, melancholy), the proportions of which determined a person's constitution and character

816–17   The formula for undoing Circe's spells (Ovid, *Met.* 14.300–01) and Busyrane's (Spenser, *F.Q.* 3.12.36)

822   Meliboeus Spenser

824 f.   The story of Sabrina—a legend of the Severn river very appropriate for a masque given at Ludlow—had been told in *The Faerie Queene* 2.10.14–19; Milton adapts it to his own purposes and theme. Sabrina, though here enveloped in classical allusions, may represent divine grace.

Dips me all o'er, as when the wrath of Jove
Speaks thunder, and the chains of Erebus
To some of Saturn's crew. I must dissemble,   805
And try her yet more strongly. Come, no more,
This is mere moral babble, and direct
Against the canon laws of our foundation;
I must not suffer this, yet 'tis but the lees
And settlings of a melancholy blood;   810
But this will cure all straight, one sip of this
Will bathe the drooping spirits in delight
Beyond the bliss of dreams. Be wise and taste.

The brothers rush in with swords drawn, wrest his glass out
of his hand, and break it against the ground; his rout make
sign of resistance, but are all driven in. The Attendant
Spirit comes in.

Spirit
What, have you let the false enchanter scape?
O ye mistook, ye should have snatch'd his wand   815
And bound him fast; without his rod revers'd
And backward mutters of dissevering power,
We cannot free the lady that sits here
In stony fetters fix'd and motionless;
Yet stay, be not disturb'd, now I bethink me,   820
Some other means I have which may be us'd,
Which once of Meliboeus old I learnt
The soothest shepherd that e'er pip'd on plains.
    There is a gentle nymph not far from hence
That with moist curb sways the smooth Severn stream,   825
Sabrina is her name, a virgin pure;
Whilom she was the daughter of Locrine,

828 Brute the great-grandson of Aeneas and the legendary founder of Britain

836 lank drooping

845 urchin ('hedgehog') caused by evil spirits (cf. *The Tempest* 2.2.5–12)

846 elf any mischievous sprite or Puck in particular (*A Midsummer Night's Dream* 2.1.33, etc.)

852 swain Meliboeus (cf. 822)

That had the sceptre from his father Brute.
She guiltless damsel, flying the mad pursuit
Of her enraged stepdame Guendolen,   830
Commended her fair innocence to the flood
That stay'd her flight with his cross-flowing course.
The water-nymphs that in the bottom play'd
Held up their pearled wrists and took her in
Bearing her straight to aged Nereus' hall,   835
Who piteous of her woes, rear'd her lank head,
And gave her to his daughters to imbathe
In nectar'd lavers strew'd with asphodel,
And through the porch and inlet of each sense
Dropp'd in ambrosial oils till she reviv'd   840
And underwent a quick immortal change,
Made goddess of the river; still she retains
Her maid'n gentleness, and oft at eve
Visits the herds along the twilight meadows,
Helping all urchin blasts, and ill-luck signs   845
That the shrewd meddling elf delights to make,
Which she with precious vial'd liquors heals.
For which the shepherds at their festivals
Carol her goodness loud in rustic lays,
And throw sweet garland wreaths into her stream   850
Of pansies, pinks, and gaudy daffodils.
And, as the old swain said, she can unlock
The clasping charm, and thaw the numbing spell,
If she be right invok'd in warbled song,
For maid'nhood she loves, and will be swift   855
To aid a virgin, such as was herself
In hard-besetting need; this will I try
And add the power of some adjuring verse.

868   Oceanus god of the river encircling the earth

872   Carpathian . . . hook the staff of Proteus

873   Triton was Neptune's trumpeter. **winding** having winding passage (cf. Ovid, *Met*. 1.333 f.)

874 Glaucus a mortal who became a sea-god and prophet

875–6 Ino became a sea-divinity under the name of Leucothea; mother of Melicertes (see note on *Lycidas* 164).

878   See note on 253.

879   Parthenope one of the sirens, who had been washed ashore near Naples and been given a tomb there

880   Ligea a name given to one of Homer's sirens

Song

Sabrina fair
   Listen where thou art sitting   860
Under the glassy, cool, translucent wave,
   In twisted braids of lilies knitting
The loose train of thy amber-dropping hair,
   Listen for dear honour's sake,
   Goddess of the silver lake,   865
      Listen and save.

Listen and appear to us
In name of great Oceanus,
By th' earth-shaking Neptune's mace,
And Tethys' grave majestic pace,   870
By hoary Nereus' wrinkled look,
And the Carpathian wizard's hook,
By scaly Triton's winding shell,
And old soothsaying Glaucus' spell,
By Leucothea's lovely hands,   875
And her son that rules the strands,
By Thetis' tinsel-slipper'd feet,
And the songs of sirens sweet,
By dead Parthenope's dear tomb,
And fair Ligea's golden comb,   880
Wherewith she sits on diamond rocks
Sleeking her soft alluring locks,
By all the nymphs that nightly dance
Upon the streams with wily glance,
Rise, rise, and heave thy rosy head   885
From thy coral-pav'n bed,
And bridle in thy headlong wave,
Till thou our summons answer'd have.
      Listen and save.

894 turkis turquoise

895 Colours that shift in the rippling water ('strays' having a plural sense)?

897 printless feet cf. *The Tempest* 5.1.34

904 band bondage

Sabrina rises, attended by water-nymphs, and sings.

> By the rushy-fringed bank,   890
>   Where grows the willow and the osier dank,
> My sliding chariot stays,
>   Thick set with agate, and the azurn sheen
>   Of turkis blue, and em'rald green
>   That in the channel strays,   895
>   Whilst from off the waters fleet
>   Thus I set my printless feet
>   O'er the cowslip's velvet head
>   That bends not as I tread.

Gentle swain at thy request   900
I am here.
Spirit   Goddess dear
We implore thy powerful hand
To undo the charmed band
Of true virgin here distress'd,   905
Through the force, and through the wile
Of unbless'd enchanter vile.
Sabrina
Shepherd 'tis my office best
To help ensnared chastity;
Brightest lady look on me,   910
Thus I sprinkle on thy breast
Drops that from my fountain pure,
I have kept of precious cure,
Thrice upon thy finger's tip,
Thrice upon thy rubied lip;   915
Next this marble venom'd seat
Smear'd with gums of glutinous heat

921 **Amphitrite** wife of Poseidon (Neptune)

923 Anchises was the father of Aeneas (see the note on 828 above)

934–5 Cf. *Arcades* 21

I touch with chaste palms moist and cold,
Now the spell hath lost his hold;
And I must haste ere morning hour   920
To wait in Amphitrite's bow'r.

Sabrina descends, and the lady rises out of her seat

Spirit
Virgin, daughter of Locrine
Sprung of old Anchises' line,
May thy brimmed waves for this
Their full tribute never miss   925
From a thousand petty rills
That tumble down the snowy hills:
Summer drouth, or singed air
Never scorch thy tresses fair,
Nor wet October's torrent flood   930
Thy molten crystal fill with mud;
May thy billows roll ashore
The beryl and the golden ore,
May thy lofty head be crown'd
With many a tow'r and terrace round,   935
And here and there thy banks upon
With groves of myrrh, and cinnamon.

Come lady while heav'n lends us grace,
Let us fly this cursed place,
Lest the sorcerer us entice   940
With some other new device.
Not a waste or needless sound
Till we come to holier ground,
I shall be your faithful guide

957 Cf. *Aen.* 3.512, 5.738, 835

960 **duck** curtsy

964 **mincing Dryades** wood-nymphs dancing daintily

Through this gloomy covert wide,   945
And not many furlongs thence
Is your father's residence,
Where this night are met in state
Many a friend to gratulate
His wish'd presence, and beside   950
All the swains that there abide,
With jigs and rural dance resort.
We shall catch them at their sport,
And our sudden coming there
Will double all their mirth and cheer;   955
Come let us haste, the stars grow high,
But night sits monarch yet in the mid sky.

The scene changes presenting Ludlow Town and the President's
Castle, then come in country dancers, after them the Attendant
Spirit, with the two brothers and the lady

Song
Spirit
Back shepherds, back, enough your play,
Till next sunshine holiday,
Here be without duck or nod   960
Other trippings to be trod
Of lighter toes, and such court guise
As Mercury did first devise
With the mincing Dryades
On the lawns, and on the leas.   965

This second Song presents them to their father and mother

Noble Lord and Lady bright,
I have brought ye new delight,

970   timely early

976–99   When the masque was acted it opened with these lines, somewhat abridged and altered. Cf. *The Tempest* 5.1.88–94 and pictures of earthly paradises in Spenser (*F.Q.* 3.6) et al.

984   crisped shades trees or bushes with leaves curled by the wind
985   spruce dainty, elegant

989   musky perfumed

995   purfl'd fringed with embroidered colors

Here behold so goodly grown
Three fair branches of your own.
Heav'n hath timely tri'd their youth,   970
Their faith, their patience, and their truth,
And sent them here through hard assays
With a crown of deathless praise,
To triumph in victorious dance
O'er sensual folly, and intemperance.   975

The dances ended, the Spirit epiloguizes

Spirit
To the ocean now I fly,
And those happy climes that lie
Where day never shuts his eye,
Up in the broad fields of the sky:
There I suck the liquid air   980
All amidst the gardens fair
Of Hesperus and his daughters three
That sing about the golden tree:
Along the crisped shades and bow'rs
Revels the spruce and jocund Spring,   985
The Graces, and the rosy-bosom'd Hours,
Thither all their bounties bring,
That there eternal Summer dwells,
And west winds, with musky wing
About the cedarn alleys fling   990
Nard, and cassia's balmy smells.
Iris there with humid bow
Waters the odorous banks that blow
Flowers of more mingled hue
Than her purfl'd scarf can shew,   995

997   Cf. 458 and *Arcades* 71–73

999–1102 Milton seems to follow Spenser's interpretation (*F.Q.* 3.6.46 f.) of
the love of Venus ('th' Assyrian Queen') as symbolising the perpetual cycle of
physical generation within the order of nature.

1000–11   These lines and 997 were added in the 1637 edition.

1003–11   Apuleius' tale of Cupid and Psyche had lent itself to Christian interpretation as representing the love of Christ for the human soul. Milton,
writing in the Platonic-Christian tradition, emphasises the Platonic love of the
good that engenders knowledge and virtue (cf. *Apology for Smectymnuus*,
quoted above, p. 197ff.). In *Comus*, which displays the victory of knowledge and
virtue, Milton makes Psyche's progeny 'Youth and Joy' ('Pleasure' in Apuleius
and Spenser, *F.Q.* 3.6.50), perhaps because Comus had claimed to embody
both, whereas they are the possession of the good.

1015   **bow'd welkin** vaulted sky

1017   **corners** horns (cf. *Macbeth* 3.5.23)

1019   Comus, who claimed to be free, is a slave to sensuality

1021   **sphery chime** the music of the spheres (above the spheres is heaven)

And drenches with Elysian dew
(List mortals, if your ears be true)
Beds of hyacinth and roses
Where young Adonis oft reposes,
Waxing well of his deep wound   1000
In slumber soft, and on the ground
Sadly sits th' Assyrian queen;
But far above in spangled sheen
Celestial Cupid her fam'd son advanc'd
Holds his dear Psyche sweet entranc'd   1005
After her wand'ring labours long,
Till free consent the gods among
Make her his eternal bride,
And from her fair unspotted side
Two blissful twins are to be born,   1010
Youth and Joy; so Jove hath sworn.
    But now my task is smoothly done,
I can fly, or I can run
Quickly to the green earth's end,
Where the bow'd welkin slow doth bend,   1015
And from thence can soar as soon
To the corners of the moon.
    Mortals that would follow me,
Love virtue, she alone is free,
She can teach ye how to climb   1020
Higher than the sphery chime;
Or if virtue feeble were,
Heav'n itself would stoop to her.

                              (1634)

Lycidas

In August, 1637, Edward King, a graduate of Christ's College and a candidate for holy orders, was drowned in a shipwreck in the Irish Sea. He was the son of an English official in Ireland, he had received some academic distinctions, and he had contributed Latin verses to academic anthologies. His youth and character and the manner of his death may have helped, along with his family's prominence, to evoke from Cambridge friends an honour usually reserved for more illustrious personages, a volume of elegies in Latin, Greek, and English, *Justa Edouardo King* (1638). Milton, who was immersed in his books at Horton (and had not written anything since *Comus* except a Greek version of a Psalm), was presumably invited to join in the memorial. He does not appear to have been a particular friend of King, although in the small world of Christ's College—some 260 students and dons—everyone would have been acquainted with everyone else; and Milton would have been remembered by the older men as a poet. *Lycidas*, signed 'J.M.', was the last and longest poem in a very mediocre collection. In the Cambridge Manuscript Milton dated it November, 1637, the month before his twenty-ninth birthday. The poem, coming near the end of the Horton period, links itself with the sonnet *How soon hath Time*, written at the beginning.

The pastoral elegy, a main branch of the pastoral genre, had its great model in Virgil's fifth Eclogue (with which the tenth, though not an elegy, went along). During the Renaissance the original Greek elegies added their influence—Theocritus' first Idyll, Bion's *Epitaph for Adonis*, and the *Epitaph for Bion* ascribed to Moschus; this last was the first elegy on an actual poet conceived as a shepherd. Renaissance poets inherited a standard though flexible set of conventions, such as the appeal to local divinities or the Muses who had not saved the dead poet, the lament of nature for its departed singer, the procession of individual mourners, and, in the Christianized tradition, the banishment of grief by the thought of resurrection and immortality. One main reason for the very long life of the pastoral convention, both in the elegy and in its other branches, was that from the beginning it had been a dramatic mask for any kind of utterance, private or public; behind an established and impersonal pattern and *persona*, the poet enjoyed complete freedom.

In the nineteenth century *Lycidas* was recognised as the greatest of pastoral elegies, but generally in a quite inadequate way; even if Dr Johnson's complaints were set aside, the poem was still a supreme neoclassical exercise. It has been only in the past generation that criticism has shown the reverberating depths and complexities of both its theme and its art, so that, for some people, *Lycidas* now stands out as perhaps the greatest short poem in English. But a brief note cannot provide more than some suggestions.

The main premise, for the Christian poet, is that the drowning of Edward King was not merely a grievous accident but a positive act of God. From that grows the central question Milton wrestles with, one of the oldest questions man had asked: 'Why should the just man suffer? How can the premature death of the good, how can the existence of evil, be reconciled with God's providence?' Milton's mother had died in the spring of 1637, but he was affected very differently by the death of a virtuous and promising contemporary on the threshold of service in God's church, the church he himself had turned away from. Milton had now spent five years in private study to prepare himself for his unknown future, for labour under his great Task-Master's eye: what if he too should be unaccountably cut off before his life's work is begun, before his entrusted talents have borne fruit? But while his personal situation helps to explain the passionate intensity of the poem, it is barely registered. In the opening lines the poet's sense of unripeness merges with the fate of young Lycidas in the general idea of unfulfilment; in lines 20–23 there are the references to 'my destin'd urn' and 'my sable shroud'; and in the lines that follow the two 'shepherds' are associated in the picture of carefree youth enjoying, with no thought of death's striking one of them, the apparent order and serenity of nature. But the personal is soon absorbed into the universal. Even pastoral nature reveals something perverse and fatal at the heart of things. Even Orpheus, the archetypal poet, was swept away. Is there any value in virtue, talent, and labour that give no promise of survival and fulfilment? What is to be the final answer is stated in lines 76–84, yet at this point it does bring assurance, and the pressure of doubt and fear continues and mounts.

The several mourners widen, in oblique terms, the questioning of God's ways. The whole poem develops in a dialectic of emotion, image, style, and rhythm, and some of the most radical contrasts lead into the climax. The harsh denunciation of the clergy, the hireling shepherds, is followed by the lyrical invocation of flowers; but this reminder of nature's beauty is ironical, a 'false surmise,' since there is no hearse to strew them on. The fact calls up the thought of Lycidas' helpless body tossing in the sea, a reminder of nature's violence that is heightened by the volume of sound. But this final note of despair yields immediately to a final affirmation, which comes now not as mere statement but with the complete assurance of a beatific vision. The sun is the grand image of death as rebirth, and 'the dear might of him that walk'd the waves' attests the divine love that envelops fragile life. The triumphant vindication of God's ways to men enables the poet to return gently to the pastoral world of order and to face the future without fear.

While the poet's conflicting emotions surge back and forth under our eyes, they are held under the most impersonal artistic control. One means toward that combined effect is the framework of the pastoral convention, which Milton re-creates and transcends. Another means is his adaptation of the pattern of the Italian canzone, the use of paragraphs and lines of irregular length and irregularly interwoven rhymes; the power of the orchestration is felt at once, though its subtleties must be studied. One formal element of the canzone, the poet's concluding address to his poem (here in *ottava rima*) becomes, as we have seen, an integral and highly significant part of the whole; it is one of Milton's great, simple, quiet endings, suggesting far more than it says.

(On the pastoral elegy, see also below, pp. 350 ff.)

   The prefatory note was added in 1645, when Anglican censorship was no longer operative (in 1638 the censor presumably had not read the poem—or lines 113–31). The changes Milton made in composition and revision are more fully recorded in such large editions as the Columbia *Works* and those of H. F. Fletcher (facsimile) and H. Darbishire.

1   There are ten unrhymed lines: 1, 13, 15, 22, 39, 51, 82, 91, 92, 161

1–2 laurels, myrtles, ivy evergreens associated respectively with Apollo, Venus, and Bacchus, and with crowns of honour, especially poetical honour (cf. *Ad. Patrem* 102, *Mansus* 6, 92)

6 dear grievous

8 Lycidas a traditional pastoral name

10 Who . . . Lycidas? Cf. Virgil, *Ecl.* 10.3 **knew** knew how. In the MS and two printed texts of 1638 Milton (apparently) wrote in 'well' before 'knew'.

15 sisters the muses. For the invocation, cf. Theocritus, *Id.* 1.64.

19 muse here a poet

26 opening 1638, glimmering

*In this monody the author bewails a learned friend, unfortunately
drowned in his passage from Chester on the Irish Seas, 1637. And by
occasion foretells the ruin of our corrupted clergy then in their
height.*

Yet once more, O ye laurels, and once more
Ye myrtles brown, with ivy never sere,
I come to pluck your berries harsh and crude,
And with forc'd fingers rude
Shatter your leaves before the mellowing year.   5
Bitter constraint, and sad occasion dear
Compels me to disturb your season due:
For Lycidas is dead, dead ere his prime
Young Lycidas, and hath not left his peer:
Who would not sing for Lycidas? he well knew   10
Himself to sing, and build the lofty rhyme.
He must not float upon his wat'ry bier
Unwept, and welter to the parching wind
Without the meed of some melodious tear.
    Begin then, sisters of the sacred well   15
That from beneath the seat of Jove doth spring,
Begin, and somewhat loudly sweep the string.
Hence with denial vain, and coy excuse,
So may some gentle muse
With lucky words favour my destin'd urn,   20
And as he passes, turn
And bid fair peace be to my sable shroud.
For we were nurs'd upon the self-same hill,
Fed the same flock by fountain, shade, and rill.
    Together both ere the high lawns appear'd
Under the opening eyelids of the morn,

29 Batt'ning feeding, fattening
30 star evening star (Hesperus); cf. *Comus* 93
30 1638: Oft till the ev'n-star bright
31 1638: burnished wheel

36 Damoetas a pastoral name, perhaps for some Cambridge don

45 canker canker-worm (cf. *Arcades* 53)
46 taint-worm some kind of parasite

48 white-thorn hawthorn

50 Cf. Theocritus, *Id.* 1.66–69, Virgil, *Ecl.* 10.9–12

52–5 Places along the west coast of England and Wales
52 steep perhaps the island of Bardsey, south of Anglesey

54 Mona the island of Anglesey
55 Deva the river Dee that empties into the Irish Sea near Chester
56 fondly foolishly

We drove a-field, and both together heard
What time the grey-fly winds her sultry horn,
Batt'ning our flocks with the fresh dews of night,
Oft till the star that rose in ev'ning bright   30
Toward heav'n's descent had slop'd his west'ring wheel.
Meanwhile the rural ditties were not mute,
Temper'd to th' oaten flute:
Rough satyrs danc'd, and fauns with clov'n heel
From the glad sound would not be absent long,   35
And old Damoetas lov'd to hear our song.
    But O the heavy change now thou art gone,
Now thou art gone, and never must return!
Thee shepherd, thee the woods and desert caves
With wild thyme, and the gadding vine o'ergrown,   40
And all their echoes mourn.
The willows, and the hazel copses green
Shall now no more be seen,
Fanning their joyous leaves to thy soft lays.
As killing as the canker to the rose,   45
Or taint-worm to the weanling herds that graze,
Or frost to flow'rs that their gay wardrobe wear,
When first the white-thorn blows;
Such, Lycidas, thy loss to shepherd's ear.
    Where were ye nymphs when the remorseless deep   50
Clos'd o'er the head of your lov'd Lycidas?
For neither were ye playing on the steep,
Where your old bards the famous Druids lie,
Nor on the shaggy top of Mona high,
Nor yet where Deva spreads her wizard stream: 55
Ay me, I fondly dream!
Had ye been there, for what could that have done?

58 f. Orpheus, the archetypal poet, was the son of the Muse Calliope; his music charmed beasts, rivers and trees; he was torn to pieces on the banks of the Hebrus by Thracian Bacchantes. Cf. Ovid, *Amores* 3.9.21.

63 Hebrus a Thracian river flowing into the Aegean Sea **Lesbian** of Lesbos, the large island near Asia Minor; cf. Ovid, *Met.* 11.15–60

66 Cf. Virgil, *Ecl.* 1.2
67 Cf. Virgil, *Ecl.* 2.14–15 **use** are wont to do
68 Cf. Virgil, *Ecl.* 1.4–5
69 Cf. Horace, *Od.* 3.14.21–22 **Or with** 1638: Hid in
70 The classic English expression of a commonplace that goes back at least to Ovid, *Ex Ponto* 4.2.36. Cf. Milton's letter sent to Diodati about the time he was writing *Lycidas* (Columbia *Works*, 12.27; Yale *Prose Works*, 1, 326 f.)
71 Another great commonplace. Cf. Tacitus, *Hist.* 4.6 (and Owen Felltham, *Resolves*, 'Of Fame'); also Boethius, *Consolatio Philosophiae* 2.7

75 The function of Atropos, the Fate who cuts the thread of life, is here given to a 'blind Fury,' perhaps to emphasise her apparent irresponsibility.

77 Cf. Virgil, *Ecl.* 6.3–4

79 glistering foil the bright setting (gold or silver leaf) of a jewel

86 Mincius a north-Italian river associated with the birthplace of Virgil (and cf. his *Ecl.* 7.12), here linked with Theocritus(the Sicilian Arethusa) as representing pastoral poetry
88 oat oaten or pastoral pipe (cf. *Comus* 345)

What could the muse herself that Orpheus bore,
The muse herself for her enchanting son
Whom universal nature did lament,   60
When by the rout that made the hideous roar
His goary visage down the stream was sent,
Down the swift Hebrus to the Lesbian shore.
   Alas! What boots it with uncessant care
To tend the homely slighted shepherd's trade   65
And strictly meditate the thankless muse?
Were it not better done as others use,
To sport with Amaryllis in the shade,
Or with the tangles of Neaera's hair?
Fame is the spur that the clear spirit doth raise   70
(That last infirmity of noble mind)
To scorn delights, and live laborious days;
But the fair guerdon when we hope to find
And think to burst out into sudden blaze,
Comes the blind Fury with th' abhorred shears   75
And slits the thin-spun life. But not the praise,
Phoebus repli'd, and touch'd my trembling ears;
Fame is no plant that grows on mortal soil,
Nor in the glistering foil
Set off to th' world, nor in broad rumour lies,   80
But lives and spreads aloft by those pure eyes
And perfect witness of all-judging Jove
As he pronounces lastly on each deed,
Of so much fame in heav'n expect thy meed.
   O fountain Arethuse and thou honour'd flood,   85
Smooth-sliding Mincius, crown'd with vocal reeds,
That strain I heard was of a higher mood:
But now my oat proceeds

89   herald . . . sea Triton. See the note on *Comus* 873.

92   What hard mishap in Spenser, *F.Q.* 2.4.16.8

96   Hippotades Aeolus, god of the winds: for 'sage,' cf. *Aen.* 1.56–66

99   Panope a sea nymph, one of the fifty daughters of Nereus

101   in th' eclipse i.e. ill-omened. In 97–101 the poet is groping in the natural world for some apparent cause of the wreck

103   Camus god of the river Cam, representing Cambridge University

106   flow'r Hyacinth, a Spartan prince loved by Apollo, whose quoit, deflected by the jealous Zephyr, killed him; from his blood came the flower, marked with the exclamation of woe, AI, AI
107   The poet is still, in pastoral terms, expressing bewilderment over an inexplicable act of God   **pledge** child (cf. *pignora*, Elegy 4.42)
109   St. Peter, the Galilean fisherman (Luke 5.3), traditionally the first bishop ('mitred locks'), to whom Jesus gave the keys of heaven (Matt. 16.19)

113–31   Milton's first attack on the Anglican clergy. In the third of his anti-episcopal tracts (*Animadversions*, 1642) he quoted the similar lines from Spenser's *Shepherd's Calendar* ('May' 103–31). Ecclesiastical satire was a traditional element of pastorals (if not of pastoral elegies); its special relevance here is that God has ended the life of the exemplary Edward King while He allows hireling shepherds to infest his church. Cf. Ezek. 34; 2 Pet. 2; Dante, *Par.* 27.19–66, 29.103–26.
114–15   Phil. 3.19; John 10.1
118   worthy . . . guest Matt. 22.8.

And listens to the herald of the sea
That came in Neptune's plea,   90
He ask'd the waves, and ask'd the felon winds,
What hard mishap hath doom'd this gentle swain?
And question'd every gust of rugged wings
That blows from off each beaked promontory,
They knew not of his story,   95
And sage Hippotades their answer brings,
That not a blast was from his dungeon strayed,
The air was calm, and on the level brine
Sleek Panope with all her sisters played.
It was that fatal and perfidious bark   100
Built in th' eclipse, and rigg'd with curses dark,
That sunk so low that sacred head of thine.
    Next Camus, reverend sire, went footing slow,
His mantle hairy, and his bonnet sedge,
Inwrought with figures dim, and on the edge   105
Like to that sanguine flow'r inscrib'd with woe.
Ah! who hath reft, quoth he, my dearest pledge?
Last came and last did go
The pilot of the Galilean lake,
Two massy keys he bore of metals twain   110
(The golden opes, the iron shuts amain),
He shook his mitr'd locks and stern bespake,
How well could I have spar'd for thee, young swain,
Enow of such as for their bellies sake
Creep and intrude, and climb into the fold?   115
Of other care they little reck'ning make
Than how to scramble at the shearers' feast
And shove away the worthy bidden guest.
Blind mouths! that scarce themselves know how to hold

123 flashy empty, worthless
124 scrannel thin and harsh (cf. Virgil, *Ecl.* 3.27)

128 wolf a traditional term of abuse in anti-Catholic writings (Matt. 7.15; John 10.12–13; Acts 20.29). Puritans especially were disturbed by what they regarded as Romanist tendencies in Laud's Church of England and by recent conversions in the circle of Queen Henrietta, a French Catholic.
129 nothing 1638, little
130–1 This, the most notorious crux in Milton, apparently means an instrument of God's justice, whatever further meanings the metaphor includes. Cf. 'the axe of God's reformation hewing at the old and hollow trunk of papacy' (*Of Reformation touching Church Discipline, Works*, 3, 1, 47) and *P.L.* 6.250–01, 317–23; cf. also Ps. 149.6–9, Matt. 3.10 and 26.31, Luke 3.9.

138 swart star Sirius, the Dog Star, associated with the parched herbage of late summer **sparely** seldom

142–50 Cf. the floral catalogue in Spenser, *April* 38 f.
142 rathe early **forsaken** in the shade, out of the sun's reach

144 freak'd splashed

A sheep-hook, or have learn'd aught else the least   120
That to the faithful herdsman's art belongs!
What recks it them? What need they? They are sped;
And when they list, their lean and flashy songs
Grate on their scrannel pipes of wretched straw,
The hungry sheep look up and are not fed,   125
But swoll'n with wind, and the rank mist they draw,
Rot inwardly, and foul contagion spread:
Besides what the grim wolf with privy paw
Daily devours apace, and nothing said,
But that two-handed engine at the door   130
Stands ready to smite once and smite no more.
  Return Alpheus, the dread voice is past
That shrunk thy streams; return Sicilian muse,
And call the vales and bid them hither cast
Their bells, and flowrets of a thousand hues.   135
Ye valleys low where the mild whispers use,
Of shades and wanton winds, and gushing brooks,
On whose fresh lap the swart star sparely looks,
Throw hither all your quaint enamell'd eyes
That on the green turf suck the honied show'rs   140
And purple all the ground with vernal flow'rs.
Bring the rathe primrose that forsaken dies,
That tufted crow-toe and pale jessamine,
The white pink, and the pansy freak'd with jet,
The glowing violet,   145
The musk-rose and the well-attir'd woodbine,
With cowslips wan that hang the pensive head,
And every flower that sad embroid'ry wears:
Bid amaranthus all his beauties shed
And daffadillies fill their cups with tears   150

157 whelming 1638, humming

158 monstrous inhabited by monsters

160 Bellerus an imaginary giant from whom Land's End (the extremity of Cornwall) might have got its Roman name, Bellerium
161 mount St Michael's Mount, off the Cornish coast
162 Places on the coast of Spain **hold** fortress
163 angel St Michael **melt with ruth** in Chaucer, *Troilus* 1.582, and Spenser, *F.Q.* 3.7.9.5–7
164 Dolphins carried to shore the dead body of Melicertes, who became the sea-god Palaemon; the Romans identified him with Portunus, the god of harbours. Cf. the story of Arion.

168 day-star the sun

173 Matt. 14.25–26

176 nuptial song for 'the marriage of the Lamb' (Rev. 19.7–9); cf. the end of the passage from *An Apology for Smectymnuus* (quoted above, p. 201)
177 This line was lacking in 1638.

181 Rev. 7.17, 21.4

To strew the laureate hearse where Lycid lies.
For so to interpose a little ease,
Let our frail thoughts dally with false surmise
Ay me!Whilst thee the shores and sounding seas
Wash far away, where'er thy bones are hurl'd,   155
Whether beyond the stormy Hebrides
Where thou perhaps under the whelming tide
Visit'st the bottom of the monstrous world;
Or whether thou to our moist vows deni'd
Sleep'st by the fable of Bellerus old   160
Where the great vision of the guarded mount
Looks toward Namancos, and Bayona's hold;
Look homeward angel now and melt with ruth
And O ye dolphins, waft the hapless youth.
   Weep no more, woeful shepherds weep no more,   165
For Lycidas your sorrow is not dead,
Sunk though he be beneath the wat'ry floor,
So sinks the day-star in the ocean bed
And yet anon repairs his drooping head
And tricks his beams, and with new spangled ore   170
Flames in the forehead of the morning sky:
So Lycidas sunk low but mounted high
Through the dear might of him that walk'd the waves:
Where other groves and other streams along
With nectar pure his oozy locks he laves   175
And hears the unexpressive nuptial song
In the blest kingdoms meek of joy and love.
There entertain him all the saints above
In solemn troops, and sweet societies
That sing, and singing in their glory move   180
And wipe the tears for ever from his eyes.

183   genius see the note on *Arcades* 26, and Virgil, *Ecl.* 5.64–65

186–93   See the end of the headnote and cf. Virgil, *Ecl.* 10.70–77

190   Cf. Virgil, *Ecl.* 1.83

192   twitch'd pulled up

193   Cf. P. Fletcher, *Purple Island* 6.77.6: 'To-morrow shall ye feast in pastures new'

Now Lycidas, the shepherds weep no more;
Henceforth thou art the genius of the shore
In thy large recompense, and shalt be good
To all that wander in that perilous flood.   185
    Thus sang the uncouth swain to th' oaks and rills,
While the still morn went out with sandals grey;
He touch'd the tender stops of various quills,
With eager thought warbling his Doric lay:
And now the sun had stretch'd out all the hills,   190
And now was dropp'd into the western bay;
At last he rose and twitch'd his mantle blue:
Tomorrow to fresh woods and pastures new.
                                        (1637)

Sonnets and Other Verse
1642—1658

Sonnets I and VII (and five Italian sonnets) belong to Milton's youth. The seventeen sonnets of 1642–58, the occasional utterances of a period given almost wholly to prose and public affairs, fall into two groups, private and public. Some of the former show Milton's genius for friendship, especially with the young. They are more or less relaxed and genial and sometimes recall Horace's urbane invitations to friends; yet even these may glance at great things and have a massive dignity. The sonnets on public men and events recall the Horace of exalted patriotic odes and the heroic sonnets of such moderns as Tasso. In Milton's hand, as Wordsworth said,

> The thing became a trumpet, whence he blew
> Soul-animating strains—alas, too few!

Such a devotee of Italian as Milton naturally broke away from the Elizabethan pattern of three quatrains and a couplet and adopted the Italian octave and sestet. But he recreated the form in English, with his eye especially, it appears, on Giovanni della Casa (whose poems he had bought in 1629). He uses run-on lines and strong medial pauses and often disregards normal word-order and a strict division between octave and sestet, so that, in spite of the rhymes—which may be, as in the *Massacre at Piedmont* (XVIII), notably sonorous and emphatic—the sonnet becomes in effect a paragraph of blank verse. In keeping with his heroic themes, Milton's style is elevated in various ways, but these ways, such as periphrasis, are functional, not inflationary.

1   colonel three syllables

8   Cf. Horace, *Od.* 4.14.1–6

10   According to tradition, the Macedonian Alexander the Great spared Pindar's house when he razed Thebes in 335 B.C.

12   repeated air the recital of the air
12–14   Plutarch (*Lysander*) says that, at the end of the Peloponnesian War (404 B.C.), the victorious Spartans refrained from destroying Athens when one of their officers sang the first chorus of Euripides' *Electra*.

Sonnet VIII

The civil war had begun on August 22, 1642. After the battle of
Edgehill (October 23), the royalist forces advanced on London,
causing great alarm; but they turned back on November 13 in the
face of a hastily mustered army. The Cambridge Manuscript recorded
two titles (which Milton did not use in print), *On his door when the
city expected an assault*, which was cancelled in favour of *When the
assault was intended to the city*. The idea of putting the sonnet on his
door was only a poetic device. It is a quite impersonal consideration,
amidst the violence of war, of the value of poetry, in terms of its
'eternising' power, as ancient and Renaissance poets often wrote of it.

Captain or colonel, or knight in arms,
   Whose chance on these defenceless doors may seize,
   If ever deed of honour did thee please,
   Guard them, and him within protect from harms.
He can requite thee, for he knows the charms   5
   That call fame on such gentle acts as these,
   And he can spread thy name o'er lands and seas,
   Whatever clime the sun's bright circle warms.
Lift not thy spear against the muses' bow'r:
   The great Emathian conqueror bid spare   10
   The house of Pindarus, when temple and tow'r
Went to the ground: and the repeated air
   Of sad Electra's poet had the power
   To save th' Athenian walls from ruin bare.

                   (1642)

2–4 The classical image of the difficult ascent of the hill of virtue (Hesiod, *Works and Days*, 287–92; etc.) is combined with the biblical image of the broad path to destruction (Matt. 7.13).

2 green Job 8.12–13, 16

5 Mary chose to listen to Jesus rather than join her sister Martha in housework (Luke 10.42). Ruth (Ruth 1) left her home in Moab for the sake of her mother-in-law Naomi.

Sonnet IX

The young girl here addressed is unknown. Among her family and friends she had evidently been regarded as a prig, and the poet gives her religious reassurance. The sonnet was presumably written later than Sonnet VIII (November, 1642) and it was included in the *Poems* of 1645.

Lady, that in the prime of earliest youth
   Wisely hast shunn'd the broad way and the green
   And with those few art eminently seen
   That labour up the hill of heav'nly truth,
The better part with Mary and with Ruth   5
   Chosen thou hast, and they that overween
   And at thy growing virtues fret their spleen
   No anger find in thee, but pity and truth.
Thy care is fix'd zealously attends
   To fill thy odorous lamp with deeds of light   10
   And hope that reaps not shame. Therefore be sure
Thou, when the bridegroom with his feastful friends
   Passes to bliss at the mid-hour of night,
   Hast gain'd thy entrance, virgin wise and pure.
                     (1642-5)

6   **dishonest** shameful (cf. Latin *inhonestus*)

8   **old man** Isocrates, the Greek teacher of rhetoric, was said to have starved himself to death after Philip of Macedon defeated Athens and Thebes at Chaeronea (338 B.C.) and reduced these city-states to subjection.

10–14   Cf. the parable of the wise and foolish virgins (Matt. 25.1–13)

Sonnet X

The Manuscript title, not used in print, was *To the Lady Margaret Ley*.
Milton's nephew, Edward Phillips, reported in his biography of his
uncle that, after Mrs Milton left him, 'Our author, now as it were a
single man again, made it his chief diversion now and then in an
evening, to visit the Lady Margaret Lee, daughter to the . . . Earl of
Marlborough. . . . This lady being a woman of great wit and ingenuity had a particular honour for him, and took much delight in his
company, as likewise her husband Captain Hobson, a very accom-
plished gentleman.' The Earl, who had held high posts under King
James and King Charles, died in March, 1629, shortly after the violent break-up of the last parliament to be held until 1640. Captain
Hobson, who married Lady Margaret in 1641, was in the parliamentary army; they were neighbours of Milton in Aldersgate Street.
This sonnet, like earlier ones, was included in the *Poems* of 1645;
it was evidently written between the end of 1642 and the end of 1645.

Daughter to that good Earl, once President
   Of England's Council, and her Treasury,
   Who liv'd in both, unstain'd with gold or fee,
   And left them both, more in himself content,
Till the sad breaking of that Parliament   5
   Broke him, as that dishonest victory
   At Chaeronea, fatal to liberty
   Kill'd with report that old man eloquent,
Though later born than to have known the days
   Wherein your father flourish'd, yet by you   10
   Madam, methinks I see him living yet;
So well your words his noble virtues praise,
   That all both judge you to relate them true
   And to possess them, honour'd Margaret.

(1642–5)

Sonnets XI and XII

Sonnets XI and XII record Milton's feelings about the attacks from Presbyterians—with whom he had allied himself in 1641–2 in writing against prelacy—on the liberal view of divorce that he urged in pamphlets of 1643–5. Like most of the sonnets that follow, they were first printed in the second edition of Milton's *Poems* (1673). In the Cambridge Manuscript (where the two are in reverse order), above 'I did but prompt' is the title *On the detraction which followed upon my writing certain treatises*, which may have been intended to cover both. These sonnets were probably written in 1645 or early 1646, since they were numbered and printed between Sonnet X (included in the *Poems* of 1645–6) and Sonnet XIII of February 9, 1646. Sonnet XI, with its colloquial style and jocose rhymes, expresses a half-humorous contempt for an age which is puzzled by a Greek title but can swallow the Scottish names that have been made familiar through Scotland's involvement in the civil war. In Sonnet XII journalistic invective includes a touch of Miltonic sublimity (6–7) and a statement (10–12) of a central Miltonic principle.

1 Tetrachordon Milton's third tract on divorce, and his fourth, *Colasterion*, were published simultaneously on March 4, 1645. 'Tetrachordon', a Greek musical term for a four-tone scale, was used because Milton was expounding, as his title page said, the four chief biblical passages on marriage and divorce.

7 spelling false misinterpreting

7–8 Mile-End Green at the east end of London

11 Quintilian (born *c.* 35 40 A.D.), the great Roman authority on rhetoric, reprehended barbarous foreign words (*Instit.* 1.5.8, etc.).

12–14 Cheke's age did not hate Greek, as Milton's does (we would say 'unlike'). Sir John Cheke (1514–57) was the first professor of Greek at Cambridge (1540–51) and tutor of Prince, later King, Edward. At the beginning and end of *Tetrachordon* Milton spoke of the reign of Edward VI (1547–53) as the 'best and purest,' 'the purest and sincerest' age of the English Reformation; the latter reference included praise of Cheke's learning and piety.

Sonnet XI

A book was writ of late call'd *Tetrachordon*,
  And wov'n close both matter, form, and style,
  The subject new; it walk'd the town awhile,
  Numb'ring good intellects; now seldom por'd on.
Cries the stall-reader, Bless us! what a word on   5
  A title-page is this! And some in file
  Stand spelling false, while one might walk to Mile-
  End Green. Why is it harder, sirs, than Gordon,
Colkitto, or Macdonnel, or Galasp?
  Those rugged names to our like mouths grow sleek   10
  That would have made Quintilian stare and gasp.
Thy age, like ours, O soul of Sir John Cheek,
  Hated not learning worse than toad or Asp,
  When thou taught'st Cambridge, and King Edward Greek.
                         (1645–6)

2   known rules See the note on Sonnet 11.1.

7   fee full possession. When Latona, with her new-born twins, Apollo and
Diana, was fleeing from the wrath of Juno, she approached a lake to get a
drink but was driven off by peasants, who were punished by being transformed
into frogs (Ovid, *Met.* 6.332–81). The 'twin-born progeny' may glance at
Milton's twin pamphlets (see Sonnet XI, note 1). Cf. Spenser, *F.Q.* 2.12.13.4–7.

Sonnet XII

I did but prompt the age to quit their clogs
  By the known rules of ancient liberty,
  When straight a barbarous noise environs me
  Of owls and cuckoos, asses, apes and dogs.
As when those hinds that were transform'd to frogs   5
  Rail'd at Latona's twin-born progeny
Which after held the sun and moon in fee.
  But this is got by casting pearl to hogs;
That bawl for freedom in their senseless mood,
  And still revolt when truth would set them free.   10
  Licence they mean, when they cry liberty,
For who loves that, must first be wise, and good;
  But from that mark how far they rove, we see
  For all this waste of wealth, and loss of blood.

                          (1645–6)

2 span join, fit. (In view of the Elizabethan composers, Lawes could hardly be called the first English musician to fit words and notes together with due regard to accent.)

4 King Midas adjudged Pan a better musician than Apollo, who thereupon changed his ears to those of an ass. **committing** forcing together (i.e. short syllables and long notes and vice versa)

10 priest . . . choir cf. Horace, *Od.* 3.1.3

11 story A note in *Choice Psalms* said that the reference was to Lawes's setting for William Cartwright's *Complaint of Ariadne*.

13 Casella Dante met the Florentine musician on the threshold of Purgatory (*Purg.* 2.76–119). Here, as elsewhere, Milton dignifies persons he admires by linking them with illustrious figures of the past.

Sonnet XIII

Henry Lawes (1595/96–1662), the distinguished court musician and composer, has been noticed already in connection with *Arcades* and *Comus*. This sonnet, which Milton dated February 9, 1646, was—according to a manuscript title—written for publication with Lawes's *Airs and Dialogues*. But the first part of this work was not published until 1653 and the sonnet was printed, with the title *To my Friend Mr Henry Lawes*, in Lawes's *Choice Psalms* (1648), a book Lawes courageously dedicated to Charles I, who was then in captivity. Lawes's royalism did not cause any breach of friendship with Milton, and Milton showed courage and magnanimity in allowing his poem to appear along with such a dedication. His tribute emphasized a quality for which Lawes's music was noted, the bringing out of the full expressive power of the words. His compositions included settings for songs by Milton (as the title page of the *Poems* of 1645 indicated) and many other poets, such as Jonson, Herrick, Carew, Lovelace and Waller.

Harry, whose tuneful and well-measur'd song
   First taught our English music how to span
   Words with just note and accent, not to scan
   With Midas' ears, committing short and long,
Thy worth and skill exempts thee from the throng,   5
   With praise enough for envy to look wan;
   To after age thou shalt be writ the man
   That with smooth air couldst humour best our tongue.
Thou honourest verse, and verse must lend her wing
   To honour thee, the priest of Phoebus' choir   10
   That tun'st their happiest lines in hymn, or story.
Dante shall give fame leave to set thee higher
   Than his Casella, whom he woo'd to sing
   Met in the milder shades of Purgatory.

                           (1646)

1 Episcopacy was formally abolished in January, 1643.

2 The Book of Common Prayer was banned in August, 1645.

3 **plurality** Milton sees Presbyterian clergymen, like a number of their Anglican predecessors, as greedily receiving the income from more than one living.

7 The system of presbyteries or regional synods (Latin *classes*) ordered by parliament would be as tyrannical as the episcopal hierarchy had been.

8 **A.S.** Adam Stuart or Stewart, a Scottish Presbyterian divine who, in London, wrote actively against the Independents. Samuel **Rutherford**, a professor of divinity at St Andrews and one of the four Scottish Commissioners who attended the Westminster Assembly, was another champion of Presbyterianism (one who, in 1649, could argue for a sort of Protestant Inquisition).

8–10 Men like the Independent divines referred to in the headnote

12 The English Presbyterian Thomas Edwards attacked the Independents' *Apologetical Narration* and the idea of toleration in *Antapologia* (1644); in *Gangraena* (1646) he catalogued and denounced many current 'heresies'.

12 **Scotch what-d'ye-call** Robert Baillie, the bitterest foe of Independency among the Scottish Commissioners

14 **packings** trickery **Trent** the Catholic Council of Trent (1545–63), which was called to combat Protestantism (and which, in *Areopagitica*, Milton saw as the main inventor of censorship)

On the New Forcers of Conscience

This specimen of a sonnet with a 'tail' or (as here) successive tails—a kind Milton knew from Italian verse—was not included in the numbered series. It was written probably in 1646. In July, 1643, the Westminster Assembly, composed mainly of divines, met under parliamentary auspices to reorganise the church on the Presbyterian model. But five Independent ministers, who wished to carry on with their own congregations, started what turned into a full-scale pamphlet debate on uniformity versus toleration or freedom of conscience. Parliamentary ordinances of 1646 established the Presbyterian system (March 14), authorized the ordination of ministers by 'classical' presbyteries within their respective bound (August 28), and abolished archbishops and bishops (October 9). But the actual results fell far short of Presbyterian hopes. Milton of course is strongly opposed to Presbyterian rigidity and intolerance.

Because you have thrown off your prelate lord
   And with stiff vows renounc'd his liturgy
   To seize the widow'd whore plurality
   From them whose sin ye envi'd, not abhorr'd,
Dare ye for this adjure the civil sword   5
   To force our consciences that Christ set free,
   And ride us with a classic hierarchy
   Taught ye by mere A.S. and Rutherford?
Men whose life, learning, faith and pure intent
   Would have been held in high esteem with Paul   10
   Must now be nam'd and printed heretics
By shallow Edwards and Scotch what-d'ye-call;
   But we do hope to find out all your tricks,
   Your plots and packings worse than those of Trent,

17   phylacteries amulets with Mosaic texts worn by pious Jews and connot-
ing hypocrisy (Matt. 23.5) **baulk** spare: a veiled reference (which in a cancelled line had been explicit) to the Presbyterian pamphleteer, William Prynne,
who in 1637, for attacking prelacy, had suffered severe punishment, including
the loss of what remained of his ears, which had been partly cut off in 1634
because of an alleged reflection on the queen
20   This famous line rests on an etymological pun, the word 'priest' being
derived indirectly from the Greek 'presbyter' (which means literally 'elder').
Milton had said similar things in *Areopagitica*.

          That so the Parliament   15
May with their wholesome and preventive shears
Clip your phylacteries though baulk your ears
          And succour our just fears
When they shall read this clearly in your charge
New Presbyter is but old Priest writ large.   20
                   (1646?)

2 Gal. 3.11

4 2 Cor. 5.1–4
5 Acts 10.4
6 Rev. 14.13

12 MS.: spake . . . in; 1673: speak . . . on

14 Rev. 22.1 and 17

Sonnet XIV

The Manuscript title is *On the religious memory of Mrs Catharine Thomason, my Christian friend, deceased December, 1646*. Her husband, George Thomason, a bookseller, earned the gratitude of modern scholars by collecting over 22,000 books, pamphlets, and newspapers of 1640–61 and dating most of them. The sonnet was evidently written in December, 1646.

When faith and love which parted from thee never,
  Had rip'n'd thy just soul to dwell with God,
  Meekly thou didst resign this earthy load
Of death, call'd life; which us from life doth sever.
Thy works and alms, and all thy good endeavour   5
  Stayed not behind, nor in the grave were trod;
  But as faith pointed with her golden rod,
Follow'd thee up to joy and bliss for ever.
Love led them on, and faith who knew them best
  Thy handmaids, clad them o'er with purple beams   10
  And azure wings, that up they flew so dress'd,
And spake the truth of thee in glorious themes
  Before the judge, who thenceforth bid thee rest,
  And drink thy fill of pure immortal streams.

(1646)

7 Hydra a many-headed serpent killed by Hercules (cf. Horace, *Od.* 4.4.61–62) **North** Although the Presbyterian Scots had made an alliance with the English parliament (the Solemn League and Covenant of 1643), negotiations with the king led to a Scottish royalist invasion in July, 1648 (see the headnote).
8 imp the grafting of new feathers to the stumps of broken ones (a traditional metaphor from falconry); hence 'strengthen'
11–14 One of Milton's many expressions of disillusionment with the Long Parliament: here, in particular, with the financial disorder and dishonesty that attended the raising of money, the confiscation and sale of royalists' estates, etc.

Sonnet XV

The Manuscript title is *On the Lord General Fairfax at the siege o,
Colchester*. Sir Thomas Fairfax, the chief parliamentary general, had
won the decisive battle of Naseby (1645). When royalists renewed
the war in 1648, Fairfax besieged Colchester. The sonnet must have
been written before the town surrendered (August 27) and also before
the battle of Preston (August 17), in which Cromwell defeated the
Scots, 'the false North' of line 7. The exhortation of the sestet was
not fulfilled: Fairfax, who did not approve of the execution of King
Charles or the invasion of Scotland, in 1650 retired into private life.
Milton praised him again in his *Second Defence of the English People*
(1654). This sonnet was first printed, along with that addressed to
Cromwell (XVI) and *Cyriack, this three years' day* (XXII), by
Edward Phillips in 1694.

Fairfax, whose name in arms through Europe rings,
  Filling each mouth with envy, or with praise,
  And all her jealous monarchs with amaze,
  And rumours loud, that daunt remotest kings,
Thy firm unshak'n virtue ever brings   5
  Victory home, though new rebellions raise
  Their Hydra heads, and the false North displays
  Her brok'n league, to imp her serpent wings,
O yet a nobler task awaits thy hand;
  For what can wars but endless war still breed,   10
  Till truth, and right from violence be freed,
And public faith clear'd from the shameful brand
  Of public fraud. In vain doth valour bleed
  While avarice, and rapine share the land.

                         (1648)

2 Ere half my days Since Milton had become 43 on December 9, 1651, this phrase would seem to stretch his expected span well beyond the Psalmist's three score and ten. He might have been thinking of his mature working life, of his father's having reached 84 or more, or possibly of Plato's hundred-year term (*Rep.* 615).

3 talent Matt. 25.14–30

7 John 9.4

11 yoke Matt. 11.29–30

Sonnet XIX

Milton's eyes had been weak from childhood and his sight began to
fail noticeably about 1644. By early 1650, when he was assigned the
task of answering Salmasius' attack on the regicides, he had nearly lost
the sight of one eye; although warned about the effect of continued
labour, he persevered. Blindness became complete in the winter of
1651-2. The dating of the sonnet has been much debated. The main
point on one side is that its place among the printed sonnets would put
composition in 1655; but in fact the sonnets are not all in strictly
chronological order, and this one seems very clearly, in substance
and tone, to express Milton's first reaction to total blindness. His
forty-third birthday was just behind him (or possibly just ahead),
and he had not yet written the heroic poem which he had put aside
at the call of public duty. The sonnet takes us back to *How soon
hath Time* of 1632, though now the parable of the talents has become
a more oppressive reality; yet Milton's faith in Providence remains
humbly steadfast. The only text of the sonnet is that of the *Poems*
of 1673.

When I consider how my light is spent,
  Ere half my days in this dark world and wide,
  And that one talent which is death to hide
  Lodg'd with me useless though my soul more bent   5
To serve therewith my Maker, and present
  My true account, lest he returning chide;
  Doth God exact day labour, light deni'd,
  I fondly ask; but patience to prevent
That murmur, soon replies, God doth not need
  Either man's work or his own gifts, who best   10
  Bear his mild yoke, they serve him best, his state

14 They i.e. angels. Milton is presumably thinking, not of two distinct orders of angels, but of all angels as God's envoys, some being sent on missions, others waiting to be sent. Cf. *P.L.* 3.648–53; Spenser, *F.Q.* 2.8.1–2.

Is kingly. Thousands at his bidding speed
   And post o'er land and ocean without rest:
   They also serve who only stand and wait.

                              (1652?)

8 Dunbar On September 3, 1650, Cromwell defeated the Scots at Dunbar in Scotland.

9 Worcester On September 3, 1651, Cromwell defeated the Scots and Charles II; Charles escaped into exile.

14 The 'wolves' (John 10.12) are not now the Roman Catholics of *Lycidas*, 128 but Puritans.

Sonnet XVI

The Manuscript title is *To the Lord General Cromwell, May 1652, on the proposals of certain ministers ot the Committee for Propagation of the Gospel*. The Committee, appointed by parliament and dominated by Independents, was considering a kind of state-controlled Congregationalism—which Milton the individualist saw as a new Established Church. The pattern of the sonnet is akin to that on Fairfax, the praise of martial prowess being followed by a summons to the works of peace, in this case the preservation of religious liberty. Milton doubtless sent a copy of the sonnet to Cromwell. It was first printed by Edward Phillips in 1694.

Cromwell, our chief of men, who through a cloud
   Not of war only, but detractions rude,
   Guided by faith and matchless fortitude
   To peace and truth thy glorious way hast plough'd,
And on the neck of crowned fortune proud   5
   Has rear'd God's trophies and his work pursu'd,
   While Darwen stream with blood of Scots imbru'd,
   And Dunbar field resounds thy praises loud,
And Worcester's laureate wreath; yet much remains
   To conquer still; peace hath her victories   10
   No less renown'd than war, new foes arise
Threat'ning to bind our souls with secular chains:
   Help us to save free conscience from the paw
   Of hireling wolves whose gospel is their maw.

                            (1652)

4   Epirot Pyrrhus, king of Epirus, invaded Italy in 281 B.C. His ambassador reported that the Roman senate was an assembly of kings. **African** Hannibal the Carthaginian, who invaded Italy in 218 B.C.

6   hollow a pun on 'Holland,' 'the Low Countries,' and the idea of subtlety or duplicity

   be spell'd understand

8 Vane had brought the navy to a degree of efficiency which made possible the victories of Blake.

Sonnet XVII

This sonnet, which Milton sent to Vane on July 3, 1652, has the Manuscript title *To Sir Henry Vane the younger*. It was first printed in George Sikes's *Life and Death of Sir Henry Vane* (1662) and then by Edward Phillips (1694). Sir Henry Vane (1613–62) was one of the ablest and most high-minded of Puritan leaders. In 1636-7, as the youthful governor of Massachusetts, he had defended the 'enthusiast,' Anne Hutchinson, against rigid orthodoxy, and in the Westminster Assembly (cf. headnote to *On the New Forcers of Conscience*) he had spoken for religious liberty. He had lately been negotiating with Dutch ambassadors who had lingered in London, although war between Holland and England had already begun, and who were given their passports a few days before the sonnet was written. As in some other laudatory sonnets, Milton enhances his subject's dignity through an illustrious historical parallel. The recognising of a clear division between church and state, for which Vane is praised, was a main article of Milton's creed. Vane was executed in 1662 by the Restoration government.

Vane, young in years, but in sage counsel old,
   Than whom a better senator ne'er held
   The helm of Rome, when gowns not arms repell'd
   The fierce Epirot and th' African bold,
Whether to settle peace or to unfold   5
The drift of hollow states hard to be spell'd,
   Then to advise how war may best, upheld,
   Move by her two main nerves, iron and gold
In all her equipage; besides to know
   Both spiritual power and civil, what each means,   10
   What severs each thou hast learn'd, which few have done.

The bounds of either sword to thee we owe.
  Therefore on thy firm hand religion leans
  In peace, and reck'ns thee her eldest son.
                                    (1652)

1 this . . . day The sonnet is being composed approximately three years after the time when Milton found himself completely blind (see the headnote on Sonnet XIX). It must therefore have preceded the *Massacre in Piedmont* (Sonnet XVIII), which could not have been composed before the end of April, 1655.

2 Milton evidently derived some small satisfaction from his not being disfigured, since he mentions the fact also in the personal passage of the *Second Defence* and in a letter of September 28, 1654, to his continental friend, Leonard Philaras; in this letter he described his symptoms and their onset.

4–6 Cf. the invocation to Light, *P.L.* 3.40–44

7 bate abate, slacken

8 bear up a nautical term for putting a ship before the wind

10 conscience consciousness

12 A pardonable exaggeration, although Milton's discomfiture of Salmasius in 1651 and Alexander More in 1654 did occasion considerable talk abroad. The manuscript has 'talks'; Phillips' version gave 'rings'.

Sonnet XXII

This sonnet dates itself (line 1) as of early 1655 (or possibly the end of 1654). It is very different in spirit and tone from 'When I consider.' Here Milton has rallied from the calamitous shock of blindness and is sustained in fortitude by the thought of his first and second *Defence of the English People* (1651, 1654) and by the 'better guide,' his faith in God's providence and the light of conscience. The sonnet was first printed in 1694 by Edward Phillips, who entitled it *To Mr Cyriack Skinner upon his Blindness*. For Skinner see the headnote to Sonnet XXI below.

Cyriack, this three years' day these eyes, though clear
   To outward view of blemish or of spot,
   Bereft of light their seeing have forgot,
   Nor to their idle orbs doth sight appear
Of sun or moon or star throughout the year,   5
   Or man, or woman. Yet I argue not
   Against heav'n's hand or will, not bate a jot
   Of heart or hope; but still bear up and steer
Right onward. What supports me dost thou ask?
   The conscience, friend, t' have lost them overpli'd   10
   In liberty's defence, my noble task,
Of which all Europe talks from side to side.
   This thought might lead me through the world's vain mask
   Content though blind, had I no better guide.

                      (1655)

1 Rev. 6.9–10

4 The sect was supposed to have originated in apostolic times. **stocks and stones** Jer. 2.27

5 **book** God's record of the righteous (Exod. 32. 32–3; Ps. 69. 28; Rev. 3.5, 20.15, 21.27)

9–10 Cf. Virgil, *Ecl.* 6.84

10–14 Cf. the parable of the sower (Matt. 13.3–9) and the myth of the warriors who sprang from the dragon's teeth sowed by Cadmus. The idea of the blood of martyrs as the seed of the church goes back at least to Tertullian, *Apologeticus* 50.

12 **triple tyrant** the pope as wearer of the triple crown and claiming the keys of earth, heaven, and hell

14 Many Reformation writers, including Spenser (*F.Q.*, Book 1), identified the papacy with the corrupt Babylon of Rev. 14.8, 17.5, 18.10. The Catholic Petrarch had done so in his Sonnet 108, which Milton partly translated in *Of Reformation*; the sonnet contained the phrase *Fontana di dolore*.

Sonnet XVIII

[*On the late massacre in Piedmont*]

This utterance was inspired by an event of April 24, 1655, when Italian troops massacred the Piedmontese 'Protestants' (known, from their medieval founder's name, Valdes, as Vaudois or Waldensians) among whom they had been billeted. In his role as Secretary, Milton drafted letters of protest which Cromwell sent to the Duke of Savoy, France, and the Protestant countries of Europe. Milton's combined invective and prayer has often been likened to the imprecations of the Hebrew prophets, and it is in fact largely cast in biblical language, harsh, compassionate, simple, and fervent. The only text of the sonnet is that of *Poems* (1673).

Avenge O Lord thy slaughter'd saints, whose bones
   Lie scatter'd on the Alpine mountains cold,
   Ev'n them who kept thy truth so pure of old
   When all our fathers worshipp'd stocks and stones,
Forget not: in thy book record their groans   5
   Who were thy sheep and in their ancient fold
   Slain by the bloody Piemontese that roll'd
   Mother with infant down the rocks. Their moans
The vales redoubl'd to the hills, and they
   To heav'n. Their martyr'd blood and ashes sow   10
   O'er all th' Italian fields where still doth sway
The triple tyrant: that from these may grow
   A hundred-fold, who having learnt thy way
   Early may fly the Babylonian woe.

                     (1655)

6 Favonius   the west wind, the Roman equivalent of the Greek *Zephyr*

12 Tuscan Florentine, Italian

13–14 apparently a playful echo of a distich in the elementary school text, *Catonis Disticha* (London, 1628), 3.5

13 spare afford, spare time to (a meaning supported by the echo of *Cato* and by the conclusion of Sonnet 21). The orthodox gloss has been 'refrain **from**'.

14 unwise The word recalls the Stoic and Epicurean ideal of the wise man who leads a disciplined life: perhaps also the parable of the wise and foolish virgins (cf. the end of Sonnet IX).

Sonnet XX

Edward Lawrence (1633–57), the eldest son of Henry Lawrence (who wrote several theological tracts and was president of Cromwell's Council, 1654–9), became a member of parliament but died before he could fulfil his apparent promise of mind and character. His virtues were praised in a poem by Sir William Davenant; and he was the recipient of four letters from the German Henry Oldenburg, a friend of Milton who later was the first secretary of the Royal Society. This sonnet was apparently composed in 1655, in the late autumn or early winter.

Lawrence of virtuous father virtuous son,
    Now that the fields are dank, and ways are mire,
    Where shall we sometimes meet, and by the fire
    Help waste a sullen day; what may be won
From the hard season gaining: time will run   5
    On smoother, till Favonius reinspire
    The frozen earth; and clothe in fresh attire
    The lily and rose, that neither sow'd nor spun.
What neat repast shall feast us, light and choice,
    Of Attic taste, with wine, whence we may rise   10
    To hear the lute well touch'd, or artful voice
Warble immortal notes and Tuscan air?
    He who of those delights can judge, and spare
    To interpose them oft, is not unwise.

                    (1655)

3   volumes *Reports* (1600 f.) and *Institutes of the Laws of England* (1628–44)

7   The Greek Euclid and Archimedes represent mathematics and science.
7 f.   Cf. Horace, *Od.* 2.11.1–4
8   Swede   The young Charles X of Sweden, nephew of Gustavus Adolphus,
spent his short reign, 1654–60, in attacks on Poland and Denmark.   **intends** in
MS.; 1673 intend   **French** French policy was at this time directed by Cardinal
Mazarin.

Sonnet XXI

Cyriack Skinner (1627–1700), grandson of Sir Edward Coke (who had been the great champion of the common law and opponent of excessive claims made for the royal prerogative by James and Charles), was himself a lawyer of liberal interests, a friend and former pupil of Milton. He has been put forward as the probable author of the early anonymous life of the poet. The sonnet was apparently composed in 1655.

Cyriack, whose grandsire on the royal bench
  Of British Themis, with no mean applause
  Pronounc'd and in his volumes taught our laws,
  Which others at their bar so often wrench;
Today deep thoughts resolve with me to drench   5
  In mirth, that after no repenting draws;
  Let Euclid rest and Archimedes pause,
  And what the Swede intends and what the French.
To measure life learn thou betimes, and know
  Toward solid good what leads the nearest way;   10
  For other things mild heav'n a time ordains,
And disapproves that care, though wise in show,
  That with superfluous burden loads the day,
  And when God sends a cheerful hour, refrains.

(1655)

1   late . . . saint i.e. the woman I lately married, now one of the blessed in heaven

3   son Hercules   **husband** Admetus

4   death In Euripides' play Death is personified as a figure with whom Heracles must contend.

6   law the ceremony for the purification of women after childbirth (Lev. 12) The reference is an external comparison which is not tied up with the precise circumstances of his wife's death.

7   once more Milton had apparently never seen his second wife, so that in his dream her face is veiled (as Alcestis' would be). When he hopes 'once more' to have 'Full sight of her in heaven without restraint,' the condensed phrasing evidently means that his present visionary sight of her will become a full reality in heaven.

9   Rev. 7.13–14

Sonnet XXIII

Milton's first wife (Mary Powell) had died in 1652. In November, 1656 he married Katherine Woodcock (b. 1628), who gave birth to a a child in October, 1657, and died in February, 1658, when she was just short of thirty; the child died six weeks later. The sonnet, one of Milton's finest, is a very moving expression of devoted love, tenderness, and reverence from a man in whom Dr Johnson and others have seen 'something like a Turkish contempt of females'. The octave is a grand and simple illustration of Milton's joining of classical, Hebraic, and Christian ideas and images.

Methought I saw my late espoused saint
   Brought to me like Alcestis from the grave
   Whom Jove's great son to her glad husband gave
   Rescu'd from death by force though pale and faint.
Mine as whom wash'd from spot of childbed taint   5
   Purification in th' old law did save,
   And such, as yet once more I trust to have
   Full sight of her in heav'n without restraint,
Came vested all in white, pure as her mind:
   Her face was veil'd, yet to my fancied sight   10
   Love, sweetness, goodness in her person shin'd
So clear, as in no face with more delight.
   But O as to embrace me she inclin'd,
   I wak'd, she fled, and day brought back my night.

                                  (1658)

Appendix

On the Ode, the Masque, and the Pastoral Elegy

The ode *On the Morning of Christ's Nativity*, the *Mask* commonly called *Comus*, and the pastoral elegy which is *Lycidas*, were composed within three literary traditions whose development in at least two instances culminates in Milton. Obviously, therefore, the greater our awareness of the antecedents which echo through Milton's lines, the greater our appreciation of his achievement. But it is imperative to remember that the study of antecedents is only a means to an end. The development of the ode, the masque, and the pastoral elegy, is often interesting, and sometimes fascinating; but it is particularly valuable when it sharpens our critical perception and thereby elicits a heightened esthetic response.

On the Ode[1]

Michael Drayton in the preface to his *Poemes Lyrick and Pastorall* (1606) conveniently reminds us of the meaning of the term 'ode' (= song), and summarises its two lines of descent from Pindar and Anacreon. In his words,

> an Ode is knowne to haue been properly a song moduled to the ancient harp, and neither too short breathed as hasting to the

[1] The best study of the development of the ode is by Carol Maddison, *Apollo and the Nine: A History of the Ode* (London, 1960). Two studies focus on developments in England: Robert Shafer, *The English Ode to 1660* (Princeton, 1918), and G. N. Shuster, *The English Ode from Milton to Keats* (New York, 1940). See also the expeditious survey by John Heath-Stubbs, *The Ode* (London, 1969).

end, nor composed of longest verses as vnfitte for the suddaine
turnes and lofty tricks with which *Apollo* vsed to menage it:
They are (as the learned say) diuerse, some transcendently lofty
and farre more high then the Epick (commonly called the
Heroique Poeme) witnesse those of the Inimitable *Pindarus*,
consecrated to the glory and renown of such as returned in
triumph from *Olimpus, Elis, Isthmus* or the like: Others among
the Greekes are amorous soft and made for chambers, as other for
Theatres, as were *Anacreon's*.

Pindar's 'transcendently lofty' odes in the first half of the fifth century
BC were composed (as Drayton accurately observes) for ceremonial
occasions like the athletic games at Olympia and elsewhere. Consistently impersonal and elevated in tone, the Pindaric ode is marked
by its extensive compass, its impressive opening lines, its deployment
of a myth at some length, and its 'cosmic' imagery. Elaborately
constructed, it depends largely on the reiteration of a dance-like
pattern of strophe, antistrophe and epode. In time, the Pindaric
ode was understood to be 'irregular' despite its regularity, 'free'
despite its strict internal discipline, and always 'lofty'.

The 'soft' ode was less the contribution of Anacreon than of two
greater poets of the seventh/sixth centuries BC, Sappho and Alcaeus.
It was from the outset 'monodic' (for single voice), in marked contrast to the later polyphonic odes of Pindar. Far shorter, it was also
far less grave, if not indeed simply light-hearted. It became, in the
first century BC, the principal object of Horace's emulous imitation,
although he borrowed the impersonal voice of Pindar even as he
introduced an ethical dimension which his predecessors lacked.
Horace in addition converted the ode into a literary composition
which, no longer intended to be sung, was enriched through a variety
of metres and verse-forms. The economy of his urbane utterance
appears to be beyond the resources of the English language, though
not necessarily beyond the abilities of Milton—witness his exquisite
translation of Horace's 'Fifth Ode' (above, p. 67).

The ode once 'discovered' in the fifteenth century by the Italian humanist Filelfo, developed thereafter by extending its range partly through the introduction of a variety of emotions, and partly through the fusion of pagan myths with Christian verities. The Horatian ode naturally continued to command respect and incite imitations, but the influence of Pindar—even, indeed, of Anacreon—can also be detected in particular instances. In seventeenth-century England, for example, Anacreon's influence proved decisive on Robert Herrick; Horace's, on Michael Drayton; and Pindar's, on Abraham Cowley. Several poets inevitably chose to write now in the Horatian vein and now in the Pindaric, notably Ben Jonson; while others— Milton among them—preferred selectively to adapt their predecessors. Milton knew Pindar well enough, or at least as well as anyone could be said to have understood Pindar's ordered 'irregularities'. His annotated copy of Pindar survives, and lately it has been argued that Cowley's *Pindarique Odes* (1656) may have contributed much to the 'irregular' verse of his *Samson Agonistes*.[1] In the ode *On the Morning of Christ's Nativity*, however, Milton adapts not so much Pindar's elaborate structures as his gravity, seriousness, 'loftiness'. Yet the result was 'a new kind of lyric in English, close and song-like, yet majestic and grandiose':

> Milton showed how the modern poet could resume the Pindaric role by choosing the most serious and universal of themes and treating them with an all-embracing knowledge. He demonstrated how learning could extend the scope of lyric poetry and give it new solidity and breadth. The medieval carol had described the birth of Christ and proclaimed our redemption. Under classical influence Milton went farther than that in his Nativity Ode. Over and over again he departed from the actual birth scene to investigate, with specific pictorial illustrations in the

[1] See Edward Weismiller, 'The "Dry" and "Rugged" Verse', in *The Lyric and Dramatic Milton*, ed. J. H. Summers (New York, 1965).

typical ode fashion, another facet of its meaning: of its meaning
to the physical cosmos and to the spiritual powers that govern it;
of its meaning to the princes of the earth; to the powers of darkness and evil; to the old religions, the old cultures, and the old
civilisations of the Mediterranean world; and to all of mankind.
With only a few allusions and pictures he made a grand synthesis
of the whole of human experience so that it all became part of
the one Christian story.[1]

The ode, unlike the masque and to a certain extent the pastoral
elegy, extends beyond Milton to include other poets of the seventeenth
century (notably Marvell), of the eighteenth (Pope, Collins, Gray,
Cowper), and of the nineteenth (Wordsworth, Coleridge, Shelley,
Keats).

On the Masque[2]

The masque is neither drama nor spectacle nor dance—nor even
literature. It is all four. But no matter how we approach the antecedents of the masque, the one element constantly within our view
is the dance.

---

[1] Maddison, *op. cit.*, pp. 329–30. Cf. Shafer, *op. cit.*, pp. 94–95.
[2] The medieval antecedents of the masque are discussed by E. K. Chambers,
The Medieval Stage (Oxford, 1903), Vol. I, Bk. II; the developments through
the 16th century, by E. K. Chambers, *The Elizabethan Stage* (Oxford, 1923),
Ch. V–VI, and especially by Enid Welsford, *The Court Masque* (London,
1927; repr. New York, 1962); the transition to the early 17th century and
Ben Jonson, by Stephen Orgel, *The Jonsonian Masque* (Cambridge, Mass.,
1968); and the period up to Milton, by J. G. Demaray, *Milton and the Masque
Tradition* (Cambridge, Mass., 1968). See also W. Mellers, *Harmonious Meeting: A Study of the Relationship between English Music, Poetry and Theatre,
c. 1600–1900* (London, 1965), Pt. II, Ch. II: 'The Genesis of Masque'. The
text of Jonson's masques is available in the edition of C. H. Herford and
Percy Simpson, *Ben Jonson* (Oxford, 1941), Vol. VII; but four of them,
with an additional ten by other poets of the period 1604–53, are now in *A
Book of Masques in Honour of Allardyce Nicoll* (Cambridge, 1967). The

Ever-present in both primitive and civilised societies, the dance was connected in ancient Greece with formal religious rituals no less than with frenzied Dionysiac revels. The line of demarcation between ritual and revels cannot be posited with assurance, for both were initially aspects of the same fertility rites; later, even after religious rituals contributed to the rise of tragedy, the actual dramatic productions were still placed under the auspices of the god Dionysus, the choral songs remaining so to speak aural reminders of the links between classical drama and the seasonal festivals of a more primitive era. But the dance also underlies later medieval festivals like the Feast of Fools and the more elaborate pageants mounted in the courts of Renaissance Europe. Man's innate love of dancing was gradually projected even to the universe at large, so that God was in time envisaged as leading the creation in a joyous dance imitated by the dancing angels, the circling stars, and the sacral play of the liturgy.[1]

The extent to which the princes of the Renaissance favoured dancing may be gathered from the enthusiastic response of Queen Elizabeth I. Even the French ambassador was impressed: 'elle dansa gayement et de belle disposition'. Her successor James I may not have participated in the rousing dances at his court, but he was a fully committed bystander. 'Why don't they dance?' he cried out once. 'What did you make me come here for? Devil take you all, dance!'

And so they did—often, we are told, in disguise, which is yet another extension of the tradition of masked dancing that reaches back to the seasonal festivals of primitive times and the dramatic

collaboration of Milton and Lawes is discussed by Willa M. Evans, *Henry Lawes: Musician and Friend of Poets* (New York, 1941), pp. 90–109.

---

[1] The fascinating story of this tradition is set forth by Hugo Rahner, *Man at Play*, trans. B. Battershaw and E. Quinn (London, 1965). See also J. C. Meagher, 'The Dance and Masques of Ben Jonson', *Journal of the Warburg and Courtauld Institutes*, XXV (1962), 258–77; reprinted in his *Method and Meaning in Jonson's Masques* (Notre Dame, Ind., 1966), Ch. IV.

performances by masked actors. Disguises were introduced to the English court by Henry VIII in imitation of Italian revels. As the contemporary historian Edward Hall reports,

> On the daie of the Epiphanie at night, the kyng with a. xi. other wer disguised, after the maner of Italie, called a maske, a thyng not seen afore in Englande . . . after the banket doen, these Maskers came in . . . and desired the ladies to daunce, some were content, and some that knewe the fashion of it refused, because it was not a thyng commonly seen. And after thei daunced and commoned together, as the fashion of the Maskes is, thei toke their leave and departed, and so did the Queene, and all the ladies.

Not infrequently the exuberance of the participants would result in a Dionysiac 'dronken maske'. But gradually order was imposed by the specially prepared dance, so expensive at times that contemporaries often protested at the 'incredible cost'. To a spectator of an Elizabethan masque it appeared as if 'they hired and borrowed all the principall jewels and ropes of perle both in court and citty'. Costumes and stage designs became increasingly more elaborate, involving expensive items such as 'gownes of crymsen Damask' for the 'pretily and richly attired' ladies, to sets with 'a Rocke of founteyne'—or even 'a goodly mount'. Magnificent scenery gradually dominated the stage to such an extent that during the reign of James I spectacle threatened to overwhelm the other elements of the masque. The intricate balance was maintained so long as poets like Ben Jonson could co-operate with stage designers like the early Inigo Jones. But during the reign of Charles I, once Ben Jonson was ostracised in favour of Inigo Jones, masques were reduced to mere spectacle. Milton's *Mask* escaped a similar fate because the poet was fortunate enough to enjoy the co-operation of Henry Lawes. The handsome tribute to Lawes in Sonnet XIII (above, p. 311) is a testimony to their amicable relationship.

The dramatic element was introduced into the masque sometime in the early sixteenth century, initially through monologues by way of comment on the action, and later through dialogue. This is not to say that the dramatic element once introduced was always retained. Only gradually did it establish itself as an indispensable part of the masque. In any case, 'drama' never meant to imply realism. On the contrary, the emphasis was from the outset on abstractions, so that the 'story' remained merely nominal, even superficial. As practised by Jonson and Milton, the masque was calculated to teach and to entertain—a twofold aim best achieved through the masque dances which should be seen as 'lessons in moral philosophy set to motion'.

The development of the masque as a literary form is by no means a straight line leading to Jonson and Milton. Each production was after all conditioned by any number of factors: the occasion, the taste of the given monarch, the emphasis on pageant or other extra-literary elements, and of course the poetic talent available at any time. Increasingly, however, the services of poets were required to write the songs and the dialogue, and finally to impose order on the overall structure. The masque as a literary form may be said to have matured by 1578, when Sir Philip Sidney presented the celebrated masque *The Lady of May*. At last, in the early seventeenth century, Jonson consolidated the various elements into unified productions which merged literature, drama, spectacle and dance. The endeavour to assert order became now explicit as

> The musicians sought to recapture the music that chimed from the heavenly bodies; the dancers to recreate the perfect movement of the planets and stars; the stage designers to link earth to the order and beauty of heaven; and the poets to reveal in flowing numbers the words of heavenly beings.[1]

Jonson was also responsible for accentuating the counter-movement known as the 'anti-masque', set in opposition to the action in the

---

[1] Demaray, *op. cit.*, pp. 28–9

masque proper. The anti-masque represents disorder, mutability, a threat to harmony. In Jonson's *Pleasure reconciled to Virtue* (1618/19), presented at the investiture of Charles as Prince of Wales, the threat of disorder is posed by the sensual Comus ('the god of *Cheere*, or the *belly*'). In Milton's *Mask* (1634), presented at the inauguration of the Earl of Bridgewater as Lord President of Wales, the anti-masque is again led by Comus. An equally interesting detail is the participation in both productions of Henry Lawes.

Milton's *Mask* was preceded by his *Arcades* which he describes as only 'Part of an entertainment' (above, p. 167). Both poems witness to the spirit of Jonson's masques. But the *Mask* is even more expressly Jonsonian, not so much in its similarities to Jonson's *Hymenaei* (1606),[1] as in its ethical orientation. Milton in 1634 stood heir to a traditional form which was essentially choreographic, theatrical, dramatic, and literary, although it was not necessarily either dance or spectacle or drama or literature. In terms of its actual treatment, however, Milton also inherited a form which Jonson had endowed with an ethical dimension. In his *Mask,* accordingly, Milton leads us to a resolution couched in the same abstract terms in which the conflict was first presented, but finally merges abstractions and reality in the dance of the participants who are no longer actors but members of the family of man.

On the Pastoral Elegy[2]

Lycidas rests on a literary tradition which, unlike that of the ode or the masque, unfolds in a direct line of development from Greek poets

---

[1] Demaray, pp. 24 ff., discerns an approximate similarity between the structural divisions of *Hymenaei* and Milton's *Mask* (the Prologue, the Anti-masque introduced by Comus, the main Masque Speeches, the main Masque Spectacle, the Resolution through the dance of the shepherds and the main masquers, and the Epilogue).

[2] The basic survey is by J. H. Hanford, 'The Pastoral Elegy and Milton's *Lycidas*', *PMLA*, XXV (1910), 403–47; reprinted in his *John Milton: Poet*

to Milton. The pastoral elegy, born in the idyls of Theocritus in the third century BC, was almost immediately extended in Bion's *Lament for Adonis* and in the *Lament for Bion* once attributed to Moschus. Virgil's eclogues, however, proved far more influential, partly because he imposed dignity on the delicate poems he inherited from 'the Greek triad', and partly because he provided the memorable lines and phrases which were to haunt the imagination of poets after him. The pastoral elegy remained static throughout the period from Virgil to the pastoral poets of the Renaissance, notwithstanding one or two interesting poems ventured during the brilliant but short-lived Carolingian revival of learning. Once Petrarch and Boccaccio turned their attention to pastoral poetry, the pastoral elegy attracted the talents of several major poets, among them Jacopo Sannazaro (1458–1530), Baldassare Castiglione (1478–1529), Clement Marot (1496–1544), and Edmund Spenser (1552–99).

Perhaps the best way to appreciate the cumulative nature of the tradition is to observe the way that details and broader 'conventions' reached Milton. Our quotations will be limited to non-English poets, however, since Spenser's *Astrophel* and *The Shepheardes Calender* (especially the 'November' eclogue) are of such crucial importance that they should be read in their entirety.

---

and Humanist, ed. J. S. Diekhoff (Cleveland, 1966), as well as in *Milton's 'Lycidas': The Tradition and the Poem*, ed. C. A. Patrides (New York, 1961). Supplementary details are provided by: George Norlin, 'The Conventions of the Pastoral Elegy', *American Journal of Philology*, XXXII (1911), 294–312; Sir John Sandys, 'The Literary Sources of Milton's *Lycidas*', *Transactions of the Royal Society of Literature*, 2nd Series, XXXII (1914), 233–64; W. P. Mustard, 'Later Echoes of the Greek Bucolic Poets', *American Journal of Philology*, XXX (1909), 245–83; M. Y. Hughes, 'Spenser and the Greek Pastoral Triad', *Studies in Philology*, XX (1923), 184–215; W. A. Montgomery, 'The *Epitaphium Damonis* in the Stream of the Classical Lament', in *Studies for W. A. Reed*, ed. N. M. Caffee and T. A. Kirby (Baton Rouge, La., 1940); *et al.* The most comprehensive anthology of poems is *The Pastoral Elegy*, ed. T. P. Harrison, with English translations by H. J. Leon (Austin, 1939), which provided most of the translations given below—except for Theocritus, who appears in the version by Andrew Lang (1880).

The echoes which reverberate through *Lycidas* can be heard in the following three instances, all of which lead us back to Virgil's eclogues:

1   Were it not better done as others use,
       To sport with Amaryllis in the shade . . . ?

Lyc. 67–8

     nonne fuit satius, tristes Amaryllidis iras
     atque superba pati fastidia?

Ecl. II, 14–15

2   Smooth-sliding Mincius, crown'd with vocal reeds

Lyc. 86

     hic virides tenera praetexit harundine ripas
     Mincius

Ecl. VII, 12–13

3   And now the sun had stretch'd out all the hills

Lyc. 190

     maioresque cadunt altis de montibus umbrae.

Ecl. I, 83

The nature of the 'conventions' inherited by Milton may be gathered in the first instance from the traditional complaint that the nymphs were absent during the tragedy (*Lycidas*, 50 ff.). The convention was introduced by Theocritus and imitated by Virgil before it became one of the great commonplaces of the pastoral elegy:

πᾷ ποκ' ἄρ' ἦσθ', ὅκα Δάφνις ἐτάκετο, πᾶ ποκα, Νύμφαι;
ἦ κατὰ Πηνειῶ καλὰ τέμπεα, ἢ κατὰ Πίνδω;
οὐ γὰρ δὴ ποταμοῖο μέγαν ῥόον εἴχετ' Ἀνάπω,
οὐδ' Αἴτνας σκοπιάν, οὐδ' Ἀκιδος ἱερὸν ὕδωρ.[1]

---

[1] *Idyl I*, 66–69: 'where, ah! where were ye when Daphnis was languishing; ye Nymphs, where were ye? By Peneus' beautiful dells, or by dells of Pindus? for surely ye dwelt not by the great stream of the river Anapus, nor on the watch-tower of Etna, nor by the sacred water of Acis'.

> quae nemora aut qui vos saltus habuere, puellae
> Naïdes, indigno cum Gallus amore peribat?
> nam neque Parnasi vobis iuga, nam neque Pindi
> ulla moram fecere, neque Aonie Aganippe.[1]

Even more persistent is the theme of universal lamentation, usually set forth through nature's desolation (*Lycidas*, 39 ff.). In *The Lament for Bion*, for instance, we read:

> σεῖο, Βίων, ἔκλαυσε ταχὺν μόρον αὐτὸς Ἀπόλλων,
> καὶ Σάτυροι μύροντο μελάγχλαινοί τε Πρίηποι·
> καὶ Πᾶνες στοναχεῦντο τὸ σὸν μέλος, αἴ τε καθ᾽ὅλαν
> κρανίδες ὠδύραντο, καὶ ὕδατα δάκρυα γέντο·
> Ἀχὼ δ᾽ ἐν πέτραισιν ὀδύρεται ὅττι σιωπῇ
> κοὐκέτι μιμεῖται τὰ σὰ χείλεα, σῶ δ᾽ ἐπ᾽ ὀλέθρῳ
> δένδρεα καρπὸν ἔριψε τᾶ δ᾽ ἄνθεα πάντ᾽ ἐμαράνθη·
> μάλων οὐκ ἔρρευσε καλὸν γλάγος, οὐ μέλι σίμβλων,
> κάτθανε δ᾽ ἐν κηρῷ λυπεύμενον, οὐκέτι γὰρ δεῖ
> τῶ μέλιτος τῶ σῶ τεθνακότος αὐτὸ τρυγᾶσθαι.[2]

which Thomas Stanley, a minor poet of the mid-seventeenth century, adapted thus:

> *Apollo* wept thy death, thy silenc'd reeds
> Satyrs Priapusses in mourning weeds
> And Fauns bewail: 'mongst woods the Nymphs that dwell
> In fountains weep, whose tears to fountains swell;
> Echo 'mongst rocks her silence doth deplore,
> Nor words (now thine are stopt) will follow more;
> Flowers fade; abortive fruit falls from the trees;
> The Ews no Milk, no Honey give the Bees,

---

[1] *Eclogue X*, 9–12: 'What groves, what glens possessed you, Naiad maidens, when Gallus was languishing with an unworthy love? It was not the mountain ridge of Parnassus or of Pindus that delayed you, nor even Aonian Aganippe'.

[2] Moschus (?), *The Lament for Bion*, 26–35.

> But wither'd combs; the sweetness being gone
> Of thy lov'd voice, Honey itself hath none.[1]

Virgil's Gallus is lamented in a similar vein:

> illum etiam lauri, etiam flevere myricae;
> pinifer illum etiam sola sub rupe iacentem
> Maenalus et gelidi fleverunt saxa Lycaei.[2]

Parallels in Renaissance literature are legion but Castiglione's lament serves as well as any:

> Heu miserande puer! Tecum solatia ruris,
> Tecum Amor et Charites periere, et gaudia nostra.
> Arboribus cecidere comae, spoliataque honore est
> Silva suo, solitasque negat pastoribus umbras.
> Prata suum amisere decus, morientibus herbis
> Arida; sunt sicci fontes, et flumina sicca.
> Infoecunda carent promissis frugibus arva,
> Et mala crescentes rubigo exedit aristas.
> Squalor tristis habet pecudes, pecudumque magistros:
> Impastus stabulis saevit lupus, ubere raptos
> Dilaniatque ferus miseris cum matribus agnos;
> Perque canes praedam impavidus pastoribus aufert.
> Nil nisi triste sonant et silvae, et pascua, et amnes,
> Et liquidi fontes tua tristia funera flerunt,
> Et liquidi fontes, et silvae, et pascua, et amnes . . . [3]

Closely related to the mourning of nature is the procession of

---

[1] *Anacreon. Bion. Moschus* (London, 1651), appended to Stanley's *Poems* (1652).

[2] *Eclogue X*, 11–15: 'For him even the laurels, even the tamarisks wept, and as he lay under a lonely crag, even pine-bearing Maenalus and the rocks of cold Lycaeus wept for him.'

[3] *Alcon*, 34–48: 'Alas, ill-starred youth! with thee has perished the solace of the fields, with thee Love and Graces, and our joys. Their tresses have fallen

mourners (*Lycidas*, 89 ff., 103 ff.). The version in Virgil's tenth eclogue reads:

> venit Apollo:
> 'Galle, quid insanis?' inquit; 'tua cura Lycoris
> perque nives alium perque horrida castra secuta est'.
> venit et agresti capitis Silvanus honore
> florentes ferulas et grandia lilia quassans.
> Pan deus Arcadiae venit, quem vidimus ipsi
> sanguineis ebuli baccis minioque rubentem.
> 'ecquis erit modus?' inquit; 'Amor non talia curat;
> nec lacrimis crudelis Amor, nec gramina rivis,
> nec cytiso saturantur apes, nec fronde capellae'.[1]

Moreover, in anticipation of the consolation, poets frequently command that the bier be decked with flowers (*Lycidas*, 134–151). Marot's

---

from the trees, the woods are spoiled of their glory and deny to shepherds their accustomed shade. The meadows have lost their splendour, shrivelling with dying grasses; dry are the springs, the rivers are dry. The sterile fields deny their promised yield, and evil mildew has devoured the growing wheat. Dismal squalor possesses the flocks and shepherds; the unfed wolf rages in the folds, and savagely tearing lambs from the udder, rends both them and their hapless mothers, and even amid the dogs fearlessly carries his booty away from the shepherds. Naught but mournful are the sounds of woodlands, pastures, and rivers, and the flowing spring wept thy sad rites, the flowing springs, woods, pastures, and rivers . . .'

[1] *Eclogue X*, 21–30: 'Apollo came and said, "Gallus, why art thou so mad? Thy beloved Lycoris has followed another amid snows and rough camps". Also Silvanus came with the rustic adornment of his head, shaking the flowering fennel and great lilies. Pan, the god of Arcadia, came, and we saw him ourselves, brilliant with the blood-hued elderberries and with vermilion. "Will there be no end of this?" he cried. "Love cares not for such deeds; cruel Love is not sated with tears nor the grasses with streams nor the bees with clover nor the goats with leaves" '.

elegy on Louise of Savoy affords one of the finest lyrical extensions
of this convention:

> Portez au bras chascune plein coffin
> D'herbes et fleurs du lieu de sa naissance,
> Pour les semer dessus son marbre fin,
> Le mieulx pourveu dont ayons congnoissance.
>   Portez rameaulx parvenus à croissance:
> Laurier, lyerre et lys blancs honorez,
> Romarin vert, roses en abondance,
> Jaune soucie et bassinetz dorez,
>   Passeveloux de pourpre colorez,
> Lavende franche, oeilletz de couleur vive,
> Aubepins blancs, aubepins azurez,
> Et toutes fleurs de grand' beauté nayfve.
>   Chascune soit d'en porter attentive,
> Puis sur la tumbe cnjcctcz bien espais,
> Et n'oubliez force branches d'olive,
> Car elle estoit la bergere de paix . . . [1]

The consolation itself is a specifically Christian contribution, however pagan the terms deployed may appear to be (*Lycidas*, 165 ff.).
Marot's formulation is within the mainstream of the Christianised
pastoral elegy:

> Non, taisez vous, c'est assez deploré:
> Elle est aux champs Elisiens receue,
> Hors des travaulx de ce monde esploré.

---

[1] *De Madame Loyse de Savoye*, 229–40: 'Bear bouquets that are full blown:
laurel, ivy, and glorious white lilies, green rosemary, abundant roses, yellow
marigold, and golden crowfoot, coxcombs coloured purple, lovely lavender,
carnations of bright hue, white hawthorns, blue hawthorns, and every flower
of great natural beauty. Let each one be mindful to bring them; then throw
them upon the tomb very thickly, and do not forget olive branches, for
she was the shepherdess of peace . . .'

> Là où elle est n'y a rien defloré;
> Jamais le jour et les plaisirs n'y meurent . . .[1]

However, it is one of the elegies by Sannazaro which has long been recognised as bearing marked similarities to *Lycidas* (172–85):

> At tu, sive altum felix colis aethera, seu jam
> Elysios inter manes coetusque verendos
> Lethaeos sequeris per stagna liquentia pisces,
> Seu legis aeternos formoso pollice flores,
> Narcissumque crocumque et vivaces amaranthos,
> Et violis teneras misces pallentibus algas,
> Aspice nos mitisque veni; tu numen aquarum
> Semper eris, semper laetum piscantibus omen . . .[2]

---

[1] *De Madame Loyse de Savoye.* 190–4: 'No, rather, be silent; there's been enough lamenting. She has been received in the Elysian fields, beyond the labours of this distressful world. There where she is, nothing has lost its bloom; never do the day and its pleasures die there . . .'

[2] *Phyllis* [Piscatory Eclogue I], 91–98: 'But thou, whether thou dost blissfully dwell in the lofty heavens, or now amid Elysian shades and the revered company of Lethe thou dost pursue the fishes in limpid pools, or dost gather with lovely finger never-fading flowers, narcissus, crocus, and long-lived amaranth, and dost blend the delicate seaweed with pale violets, look down upon us and graciously come to us; ever shalt thou be goddess of waters, ever a glad token for fishermen . . .'

Annotated Reading List

🎏🎏🎏🎏🎏🎏🎏🎏🎏🎏🎏🎏🎏🎏🎏🎏🎏🎏🎏🎏🎏🎏🎏🎏🎏🎏🎏🎏🎏

Several annual bibliographies list the latest studies of Milton: *The English Association's The Year's Work in English Studies*; the Modern Humanities Research Association's *Annual Bibliography of English Language and Literature*; *Publications of the Modern Language Association of America*; *Studies in Philology*; and *Milton Quarterly*. There are comprehensive annotated bibliographies in Douglas Bush, *English Literature in the Earlier Seventeenth Century* (Oxford, 2nd edn., 1962), and C. A. Patrides, ed., *Milton's Epic Poetry* (Penguin Books, 1967).

The standard edition is *The Works of John Milton*, gen. ed. F. A. Patterson (Columbia Univ. Press, 1931–40), 20 vols.; in part being superseded by the scholarly edition of the *Complete Prose Works of John Milton*, gen. ed. D. M. Wolfe (Yale Univ. Press, 1953 ff.) 7 vols. There are fully annotated one-volume editions of the poetry by M. Y. Hughes (1957), Douglas Bush (1965), John Carey and A. D. S. Fowler (1968) *et al*. The best edition of Milton's sonnets is by E. A. J. Honigmann (1966).

The best critical biographies of Milton are by E. M. W. Tillyard (1930), J. H. Hanford (1949), David Daiches (1957), Emile Saillens (1959, translated 1964), and Douglas Bush (1964). The most magisterial work is W. R. Parker's *Milton: A Biography* (Oxford, 1968) 2 vols.

Collections of Essays

Barker, A. E. (ed.) *Milton: Modern Essays in Criticism* (1964). Contains ten useful essays on the Minor Poems.

Critical Essays on Milton from ELH (1969). Contains three excellent essays on *Comus*.

Diekhoff, J. S. (ed.) *A Maske at Ludlow: Essays on Milton's 'Comus'* (1968). Eleven essential studies, with an extensive bibliography.

Patrides, C. A. (ed.) *Milton's 'Lycidas': The Tradition and the Poem* (1961). Fourteen studies of fundamental importance, with an extensive bibliography.

Safer, E. B. and T. L. Erskine (eds.) *L'Allegro and Il Penseroso* (1970). Fifteen essays and extracts on the twin lyrics.

Summers, J. H. (ed.) *The Lyric and Dramatic Milton* (1965). Contains three significant essays on 'the rising poet', on *Comus*, and on *Lycidas*.

General Studies

Arthos, John *On a Mask presented at Ludlow Castle* (1954). On the imaginative forming of *Comus* in the light of its sources.

Brooks, Cleanth, and J. E. Hardy 'Essays in Analysis' in *Poems of Mr John Milton* (1951). Studies of all the Minor Poems.

Gordon, George 'The Youth of Milton' in *The Lives of Authors* (1950). Three graceful lectures on Milton's early development.

Hanford, J. H. 'The Youth of Milton: An Interpretation of his Early Literary Development' in *John Milton: Poet and Humanist* (1966).

Leishman, J. B. *Milton's Minor Poems* ed. G. Tillotson (1969). With important essays on *L'Allegro, Il Penseroso, Arcades, Comus, Lycidas*, etc.

Nelson, Lowry, Jr. *Baroque Lyric Poetry* (1961). Focuses on the poetic practice of Donne, Milton (in the *Nativity Ode* and *Lycidas*), and select Continental poets.

Nicolson, M. H. *A Reader's Guide to John Milton* (1964). Introductory.

Prince, F. T. *The Italian Element in Milton's Verse* (1954). With excellent chapters on *Lycidas* and the sonnets.

Rajan, B. *The Lofty Rhyme* (1970). With three discriminating essays on the *Nativity Ode*, *Comus*, and *Lycidas*.

Tuve, Rosemond *Images and Themes in Five Poems by Milton* (1957). Very important essays on the *Nativity Ode*, *L'Allegro*, *Il Penseroso*, *Comus*, and *Lycidas*.

Individual Essays

Barker, A. E. 'The Pattern of Milton's *Nativity Ode*' in *Milton: Modern Judgements* ed. A. Rudrum (1968). A basic study.

Broadbent, J. B. 'The Nativity Ode' in *The Living Milton* ed. Frank Kermode (1960).

Broadbent, J. B. *Milton: 'Comus' and 'Samson Agonistes'* (1961). Introductory.

Brockbank, Philip 'The Measure of *Comus*', *Essays and Studies* n.s. XXI (1968), 46–61. On the poem's appeal to 'the ethical imagination'.

Carpenter, N. C. 'The Place of Music in *L'Allegro* and *Il Penseroso*' *University of Toronto Quarterly* XXII (1953), 354–67. Music is said to clarify the form, content and meaning of the twin lyrics.

Carrithers, G. H. 'Milton's Ludlow *Mask:* From Chaos to Community' *ELH: Journal of English Literary History* XXXIII (1966), 23–42. The poem's movement is primarily from 'threatened isolation' to 'charitable commitment'.

Cope, J. I. 'Fortunate Falls as Form in Milton's *Fair Infant*' *Journal of English and Germanic Philology* LXIII (1964), 660–74. The best study of a neglected poem.

Garrod, H. W. 'Milton's Lines on Shakespeare' *Essays and Studies* XII (1926), 1–23.

Seaton, Ethel '*Comus* and Shakespeare' *Essays and Studies* XXXI (1945), 68–80. Argues the influence of *Romeo and Juliet*.

Sherburn, George 'The Early Popularity of Milton's Minor Poems' *Modern Philology* XVII (1919–20), 259–78, 515–40. On the critical views expressed to 1740.

Spitzer, Leo 'Understanding Milton' in *Essays on English and American Literature* ed. A. Hatcher (1962). Argues that Sonnet XXIII is 'perfectly understandable' without the theory of Milton's blindness.

Stoehr, Taylor 'Syntax and Poetic Form in Milton's Sonnets' *English Studies* XLV (1964), 289–301. The 'particularly moving quality' of the sonnets resides in Milton's ability to match sound and sense.

Svendsen, Kester 'Milton's Sonnet on the Massacre in Piedmont' *Shakespeare Association Bulletin* XX (1945), 147–55.

Williams, Charles 'Introduction' to *The English Poems of John Milton* (1940); reprinted in *Milton Criticism* ed. J. Thorpe (1950). An influential essay, with an important reading of *Comus*.

Woodhouse, A. S. P. 'Notes on Milton's Early Development' *University of Toronto Quarterly* XIII (1943), 66–101. A survey.

See also the studies cited above, pp. 343, 346–7, 350.